TEACH
ONLY LOVE

TEACH ONLY LOVE

The Seven Principles
of Attitudinal Healing
by
Gerald G. Jampolsky, M.D.
Author of Love Is Letting Go of Fear

BANTAM BOOKS
Toronto • New York • London • Sydney • Auckland

TEACH ONLY LOVE

A Bantam Book / October 1983

2nd printing . . . December 1983

Library of Congress Cataloging in Publication Data

Jampolsky, Gerald G., 1925–
 Teach only love.

 1. Mental healing. 2. Attitude (Psychology)
3. Love. I. Title.
RZ401.J34 1983 616.89'14 83-90656
ISBN 0-553-34007-7 (pbk.)

Published simultaneously in the United States and Canada

---

*Bantam Books are published by Bantam Books, Inc. Its trademark,
consisting of the words "Bantam Books" and the portrayal of a rooster,
is Registered in the United States Patent and Trademark Office and in
other countries. Marca Registrada. Bantam Books, Inc., 666 Fifth
Avenue, New York, New York 10103.*

PRINTED IN THE UNITED STATES OF AMERICA

S   11 10 9 8 7 6 5

This book is dedicated to my dear friends, Gayle and Hugh Prather. It was Gayle who gave the name to this book, made numerous editorial suggestions and spent countless hours retyping the manuscript; and it was Hugh who came to my rescue by rewriting the manuscript. I am forever grateful for their presence in my life, for their unconditional love, help and support, as well as for their willingness to see the light within me even at those times when I do not seem able to see or experience that light myself.

 CONTENTS

ACKNOWLEDGMENTS

I wish to express my thanks to William Thetford, Jules Finegold, Mary Abney and Patricia Hopkins for their loving support and their editorial assistance. I also want to thank Grace Bechtold, senior editor at Bantam Books, for her patience, perseverance, and encouragement.

I am very grateful to Judy and Bob Skutch of The Foundation for Inner Peace for their permission to quote from A *Course in Miracles*. And, above all, I am grateful for the inspiration and influence of A *Course in Miracles* on this book.

❧ INTRODUCTION

As we emerge from the birth canal, we enter the world desperately struggling for breath. Most of us travel through life continuing to struggle, feeling unloved and alone. All too often we are afraid. Afraid of sickness and death, afraid of God, even afraid of continuing to live. Often we leave the world the same way we entered it—desperately struggling for breath.

I believe there is another way of looking at life that makes it possible for us to walk through this world in love, at peace and without fear. This other way requires no external battles, but only that we heal ourselves. It is a process I call "attitudinal healing," because it is an internal and primarily mental process. Properly practiced, it will, I believe, allow anyone, regardless of his circumstances, to begin experiencing the joy and harmony that each instant contains, and to start his journey on a path of love and hope.

The mind can be retrained. Within this fact lies our freedom. No matter how often we have misused it, the mind can be utilized in a way that is so positive that at first it is beyond anything we can imagine. However, before the mind is retrained, it may seem to be composed of tightly locked compartments. We sense our potential, but it is held behind "closed doors." As you will begin to see as we progress on our journey together, these blocks are really only attitudes in need of healing, and because they are attitudes that we alone have chosen, they can be altered. With each small change, another "door" springs open. At the start, we feel trapped and unable to escape our limitations, but as each unhelpful attitude is put aside, we see more clearly that our mind was never meant to be compartmentalized in any way. All our potential has always been at hand because our mind *is* whole. And the only barriers to our happiness are self-imposed.

Our attitudes determine whether we experience peace or fear, whether we are well or sick, free or imprisoned. Love, in its true meaning, is the attitude that this book is about. <u>Love is total acceptance and total giving—with no boundaries and no exceptions</u>. Love, being the only reality, cannot be transformed. It can only extend and expand. It unfolds endlessly and beautifully upon itself. Love sees everyone as blameless, for it recognizes the light within each one of us is. <u>Love is the total absence of fear and the basis for all attitudinal healing</u>.

If, like me, you are still struggling and want to escape from pain, depression, sorrow and anxiety so that you may experience love, then we can be sure it is no accident you and I have found each other through this book. I will be writing to you about the approach I am trying to apply more consistently to my own life. It is also the one on which I founded The Center for Attitudinal Healing. I will be telling you some of the many ways that the children who have come there have taught me love, and how you and I can avail ourselves of that love in any difficulty that may arise.

GERALD G. JAMPOLSKY, M.D.
May, 1982
Tiburon, California

TEACH
ONLY LOVE

CHAPTER ONE

THE ONLY LESSON IS LOVE

There is really only one lesson to learn. But it can be stated many ways. One of the ways that I personally find meaningful comes from A *Course in Miracles*.*

Teach only love, for that is what you are.

This statement indicates both our goal and the means to achieve it. It tells us that our essence is love. And it tells us how to recognize this in any difficulty, large or small: give only love; teach only peace; and never turn to attack in any form for your safety. This is the first and overall principle of attitudinal healing.

I have lost sight of this truth many times in my life. Yet it is encouraging how the simple truth keeps reappearing. In the spring

*This and all subsequent quotations from A *Course in Miracles*, are reprinted by courtesy of The Foundation for Inner Peace, P.O. Box 635, Tiburon, CA 94920. Copyright © 1975.

of 1975, many of the things that I was beginning to believe might be true became clearer. It was then that I was given A *Course in Miracles*. Prior to that time I had come to recognize certain "realities," but I had not put these tantalizing facts into a consistent whole. The following summary of what I had become aware of prior to my encounter with A *Course in Miracles* could be called my first glimmerings of the principles of attitudinal healing.

When someone is occupied with helping another person, he experiences no fear.

Fear does not bring about positive change. It is a mistake to provoke fear in an attempt to help others.

We cannot successfully hide our fears from children.

The true contents of our minds are open to all, especially children, and on one level all minds are in communication.

We are not confined to our bodies, and we are not limited by physical reality.

The mind, through its will to live, can affect the course of an illness. There is no irreversible difficulty.

A preoccupation with the past disturbs our present attitudes.

We can always learn from any situation we are currently involved in, no matter how undesirable it may first appear.

Our inner goals determine our experience. We are not a victim of the world.

Love does exist.

I would like to share with you some of the experiences that led me to these conclusions. By seeing specifically how I learned to apply the lessons of love, you will, I hope, be able to make similar connections in your own life. I believe that what life is allowing us to discover is how to transfer what we see clearly and simply in one part of our experience to those areas where fear still seems reasonable to us.

THE TRUTH REPEATS ITSELF

"Yesterday was awful, today is terrible and tomorrow will be even worse." That is the way my family looked at life when I was a boy. I suspect there may also have been a little of this attitude around when you were growing up. From generation to generation, we have all been steeped in the belief that the past predicts the future and that a mature person of good judgment carefully considers the lessons of the past when laying his plans. A *Course in Miracles* points out that the past has only one lesson to teach us:

This Instant is the only time there is.

The belief that the past provides the true laws of life enters our minds in an even more subtle way than through our direct attempts to control what is to come. We constantly think about the future and *expect* it to be like the past. Our fantasies and idle thoughts attempt to project into the future what we remember having liked in the past and to see eliminated what was difficult and painful.

What we are doing when we think in this way is not to look ahead in a practical and reasonable manner, but merely to make for ourselves a mental state that is composed almost entirely of fear. We believe that the general turn of the events in our lives is not to be trusted, and so we view everyone and everything either as an enemy or at least as potentially dangerous. This attitude, in turn, makes us feel unworthy of love. It makes us feel guilty and helpless and ambiguous about everything. It results in an attempt to control reality, and so the only talents we develop are manipulative ones.

This, of course, is the very mistake I myself have made so often. I tried to present myself to the world in a way that was quite different from how I was feeling inside. Inside, I may have been scared about what was going to happen, but outside I wore the costume of a man who was in control and to be respected. As is true of anyone who wears a mask, I felt isolated and misunderstood.

When we do not feel loved or lovable, we usually make the mistake of trying to gain control over the external circumstances we believe are causing our unhappiness. Because this goal requires the future in which to be fulfilled, the present moment is devalued. Even a dismal future over which we have some control seems preferable to this moment. And happiness, which requires that our full attention be on the present, becomes fearful. If some degree of happiness should occur, anyone with this attitude would immediately become suspicious of it. Fear stimulates an unconscious desire to be unhappy in order that we may focus on and control the future. Whenever we are afraid, we think we see value in keeping the present free of all love and enjoyment.

With this attitude, I not only felt unloved but unworthy of love. I was unworthy because I felt guilty of some unnamed sin. And because of my fear that my sin would be punished, I believed I had to sacrifice love in order to ward off punishment. One does not need to have had religious training to believe he has to suffer.

Most of us feel very much alone in the particular ways we make mistakes. We think our guilt is private. I thought I owned the biggest stockpile of guilt in the world, and consequently, calamity seemed always to lurk just around the corner. Life was an outside force against which my own wits and energies were pitted. Living, in the true sense of the word—with zest, peace, joy and harmony—seemed possible only for others. Wearing a mask myself, I believed what other people's masks communicated: They could be happy; I could not.

This general attitude resulted in existing but not in living. More often than not, I confused happiness with pain, for I only felt alive when I was in the midst of a crisis. Therefore, I precipitated crisis after crisis. Since happiness itself seemed out of reach, this was the only way I knew to experience life. And as these adversities kept assaulting me, this approach seemed more and more a simple necessity. I was merely a victim.

For much of my life, I believed that this outlook came to me naturally. Because of the genes I had received from my parents and the environment in which I had grown up, I had become, through no choice of my own, fearful and guilt-ridden. It did not occur to me that the choice between love and fear was mine to make instant by instant. There are many people who came from surroundings much worse than mine who have chosen not to get stuck in their pasts. I chose to buy into my parents' philosophy and accept the limitations of my environment.

It is now clear to me that each one of us determines the beliefs by which he lives. We think we must identify with our past but this is not so. We have an alternative. Our world is not held together by our worrying about it. We can lead a life that is free of fear. Just as I am, you are the determiner of everything that happens to you. This fact should not make us feel guilty, it should instead provide freedom to be at peace.

This was made evident to me during my third month of internship. In 1945, as part of the Navy's V-12 unit, I was sent to Stanford University Medical School and was released from the Navy a year later to continue my medical education. In medical school, it seemed that nearly a third of the class experiences symptoms of whatever disease was being studied. Some even come down with it. I was especially afraid of tuberculosis and was convinced I would eventually contract it and die, and as it turned out, during my intern year, one of my assignments was to the tuberculosis ward. I had a recurring fantasy that I would take one deep breath in the morning and not breathe for the rest of the day.

One night, I was called on ward emergency for a fifty-year-old woman alcoholic who had tuberculosis and cirrhosis of the liver. She was bleeding from her esophagus, had vomited blood and was in shock. Her pulse was feeble and her blood pressure not measurable. I siphoned the blood from her throat and gave her cardiac massage. That night something was wrong with the oxygen machine, so I had to give her mouth-to-mouth resuscitation, to which she responded favorably.

When I returned to my quarters and looked at myself in the mirror, my green surgical gown was a bloody mess. Suddenly, it occurred to me that not once during that hectic hour had I been afraid. It was a powerful lesson to realize that when I focused only on helping, I had no fear. There were other times during my assignment to that ward when I was evaluating what I was getting or not getting, that I was immobilized with fear. The lesson was clear. When a person is concerned only with giving, there is no anxiety. Much later in my life, I was to discover that very often there is also no pain or sense of limitation.

MINDS COMMUNICATE

I had another important learning experience that same year, taught to me by an eight-year-old boy named Billy: We can't hide our emotions from children no matter how hard we try. Thoughts that hurt us cannot be concealed, but they can be changed. Here are two quotes from A Course in Miracles that throw light on this lesson:

> I have said that you cannot change your mind by changing your behavior, but I have also said, and many times, that you can change your mind.

Later, the Course adds that

> when someone truly changes his mind, he has changed the most powerful device that was ever given him for change.

This is true whether we think it is our behavior or another's that is the problem. The mistake I made in the incident involving Billy was to attempt to change him, rather than concern myself with my own inner healing. When the mind accepts healing, that improved state will of itself extend to all the other minds with which it is joined.

Billy had not only cerebral palsy but also a behavior problem. As a psychotherapist, I had been seeing him and his parents, but rather than things getting better, they had gotten worse. One day his parents expressed their disappointment to me. I began to feel resentment toward Billy for making me look bad. Either resentment or pride is what results when our goal is to change someone.

That night I read an article by Milton Erickson, the father of modern hypnosis in the United States. It described using hypnosis with children. Apparently, all that was necessary was to relax the child, give a few suggestions and, presto! behavior would be changed. Part of me had doubts about the method, yet another part was desperate enough to try it.

The next time I saw Billy, I had him sit on the hospital gurney and I gave him suggestions that his eyes were getting heavier and heavier, that his eyes were closing because they were so heavy, and that he was lying down on the gurney. Imagine my surprise when he did everything I suggested. He was cooperating perfectly, something he had never done before. But suddenly he sat up. His eyes were closed but he leaned over and put his nose against mine and said in his thick-tongued, palsied speech, "Dr. Jampolsky, your eyes are getting heavier and heavier." Then he broke out laughing.

After I recovered from the shock, we had a good laugh together. Kids are great therapists because they have not had the kind of formal teaching that can sometimes interfere with our deep intuitive knowledge. They know what is going on in an adult's heart. Instinctively, they seem to recognize that there is nothing hidden or secret; and they usually see through any mask we wear.

AN ATTITUDE CAN HEAL

In 1949, while interning in Boston, I became fully aware of the influence that attitudes have on the body. This recognition was brought forcefully to mind by two patients under my care who had stomach cancer. Medical consultants from Boston, Harvard and Tufts Universities agreed that both men, about the same age, had similar involvement and that neither could be expected to live more than six months. One of the men died two weeks later. The other continued to live, was dismissed from the hospital and was doing well at the time I completed my internship.

The first man seemed to have no reason for living. He believed that even if he recovered there would be no way to resolve his day-to-day problems. He seemed more afraid of living than of dying. Death may have been an escape for him. The man who did not die had a determination to live; in effect, he refused to become a statistic on an insurance probability curve. Somehow, someway, he was convinced he would get well and would be able to complete the plans for his life.

This incident made me realize the importance of the thoughts we think. The direction they take actually constitutes our will to live or die. It is important to understand, however, that whenever I speak of a change in thought, I am not calling you to battle. The means whereby we redirect the mind are identical to the nature of the new direction itself. Peacefully we return to peace. Gently we lean into gentleness. If ever you find yourself unwilling to think the kind of thoughts that you believe this book calls for, please do not fight yourself. It is a letting go of tension that is being recommended. If you will simply think what it pleases you to think, what rests and comforts you, you will be doing all I suggest. There is no rationale in trying to force a change in your state of mind. Simply take careful notice of what it is that makes you happy to think, and what makes you unhappy, and your mind will make the necessary adjustments itself.

It is clear to most physicians that attitude can affect organic illness. They know that the will to live or die can change the course of an illness. They know this though such an attitude cannot be put under a microscope, measured, weighed, or replicated. The truths of the mind defy the usual standards of science. The conditions and general atmosphere produced by our attitudes can be seen reflected not only in the extreme case of life-threatening illness but in all aspects of our lives. This became clear to me after my first attempt to pass my boards in psychiatry and neurology.

Taking the boards requires two days of oral testing. Although I had studied hard, I made the mistake of deciding I would be the calmest, coolest person ever to take the exams. My central focus was on wearing such a mask, and everyone, especially my professional associates, marveled at my composure. A month later, I learned that I had failed. All my energy had gone into pretending to be in control, and this left very little attention that could be directed to answering the questions properly. The following year, without this distracting pretense, I took the exams and passed.

In 1952, I joined the staff as a Fellow at Langley Porter Institute in San Francisco. My work there involved seeing children who were schizophrenic. Most of these youngsters were unable to speak and the work was difficult, but I did begin to at least sense one important fact: Words are irrelevant to what we teach and learn.

The *experience* of love and peace is the only thing of importance that is communicated. It is this attitude of the heart and not what is said between two people that does healing work in both directions. One party's accumulation of verbal knowledge is of little use to deep inner healing.

My fellowship was interrupted when the Korean conflict broke out and I was called into service with the Air Force. After the service, I returned to Langley Porter to finish my fellowship in child psychiatry, and it was not long after this that I began to observe something that indicated that, along with words, training and experience are also of questionable value.

It became apparent to me that second-year medical students were often more proficient with their patients than were third-year residents. This assumption led me to a discussion with Ethel Vergin, who at that time was the administrative head of the outpatient department. She was a keen observer of the medical staff and had seen many medical students, residents and consultants come and go during her more than fifteen years at the Institute. She confirmed my observation.

I began to wonder why this discrepancy existed. It occurred to me that attitudes might be the primary factor, so I began examining the personality and performance of each individual resident I worked with. My study confirmed that in the handling of difficult illnesses, third-year residents, usually showed little or no improvement over those with less experience. For instance, third-year residents treating patients diagnosed as chronic schizophrenics learn from many consultants that treatment of this disease is tedious and frequently very slow. So, when these residents see a new patient with chronic schizophrenia, they have already incorporated the values and attitudes of the consultants into their own thinking. They begin the patient's treatment with the expectation that progress will be protracted and difficult. The patient in turn identifies with the resident's limited expectation and this becomes the reality.

Second-year medical students, who have not been contaminated by the negative experiences of many medical consultants, are usually enthusiastic and optimistic about seeing their first psychiatric patients. The label given to the patient means little to them. They just know that one way or another they are going to help the patient and that progress will be made. The patient identifies with this positive expectation and often improves more rapidly than with the third-year resident. In this particular situation, it is clearly one's attitude that is of paramount importance and not one's experience. In fact, experience in this instance can even be viewed as a hindrance. This taught me to never decide in advance what is best for another person, and not to consider any human being as simply a predetermined statistic.

Far more often than we realize, we see only the past in the people we encounter. But it is actually *our* past rather than theirs that we view as part of them. Consequently, we do not respond to them, but only to our various preconceptions. The kind desire to see others as they are this instant will go a long way toward purifying our attitudes. There would be very little to dislike in other people if we refused to bring to them all of our own judgments and petty grievances. Our past experiences cannot tell us of present love. Remembering and seeing are not the same, and that is why memories are of little use to us in forming loving relationships.

LOVE EXISTS

As my personal search continued, I became interested in Kirlian photography, which some investigators think depicts the electrical energy that surrounds all physical bodies. My research in this area led to an unusual experience with the Indian guru Swami Muktananda, whom I had heard of but never met. In 1974, I was invited to his Oakland ashram to take Kirlian photos of his hands.

There were many young people at the ashram when I arrived, and they seemed to idolize Baba. At that time in my life, I was very judgmental toward gurus. I quickly concluded that these young people were emotionally mixed-up and probably had father fixations. It seemed likely that they found the ashram a safe place to be because they were unable to function in the real world.

Soon after my arrival, I was seated in a room with twenty invited guests. Baba entered; we were introduced, and conversed through an interpreter. I took some photographs, was brushed by him with a long peacock feather, and sat down. As I observed others, I realized I had done everything wrong. Everyone else knelt before speaking to him; everyone, except me, had brought him flowers, fruit or some kind of gift.

My mind ran wild with hostility. Yet I had the sudden and distinct impression that, although Baba was talking aloud to others, he was having a non-verbal conversation with me. It was as though our minds were joined. I sensed with certainty that when he was finished speaking with the others, he would approach me, touch my face, and something very dramatic would happen.

He finished speaking and started to leave the room, and I said to myself, "Wrong again, Jampolsky." Suddenly, he was standing in front of me with his interpreter. He touched me, and everyone else in the room became excited. I was led to a small room and told I would be left alone for a short period and that I should spend the time meditating. I was still suspicious but, as there seemed nothing to lose, I went along with the suggestion.

Then I had one of the strangest and most amazing experiences in my life, an experience which resulted in a radical shift in my belief system. After sitting quietly for five minutes, my body began to quiver and shake in an indescribable manner. Beautiful colors appeared all around me, and it seemed as though I had stepped out of my body and was looking down at it. Part of me wondered if someone had slipped me a hallucinogenic drug or if I was going crazy.

I saw colors whose depth and brilliance were beyond anything I had ever imagined. I began to talk in tongues—a phenomenon I had heard about but discredited. A beautiful beam of light came into the room and I decided at that moment to stop evaluating what was happening and simply be one with the experience, to join it completely.

That was the last thing I remember until Baba's interpreter began shaking me and apologizing profusely, saying they had forgotten they had left me in the room. I was still in the sitting position. Two and a half hours had slipped by. I was taken downstairs where there were about 200 people in front of Baba. Everyone made room for me, and he and I had a conversation.

Someone took a picture of me which I still have. I look like a male Mona Lisa with eyes of light and a smile hiding a secret.

Baba suggested that I obtain a picture of his guru and meditate in front of it. I chose not to do this. I did pick up a small book in which I discovered that all the things I had experienced were described.

Although I usually have a high energy level, for the next three months it was heightened and I required very little sleep. I was filled with an awareness of love unlike anything I had known before. The power of this experience made me want to take a new look at everything I was calling real, because I had glimpsed a reality that is not limited to the physical plane. This was an important step toward a complete reappraisal of my concepts about God and spirituality. Although I didn't know it at the time, this experience was to prepare me for my encounter with A *Course in Miracles* a year or so later. But in the meantime, I was still struggling.

CHAPTER TWO

HELP
IS ALREADY
HERE

In the last chapter, I talked about how truth keeps reappearing. I can remember a time when as a boy of four or five I was lying on the grass, looking at the flowers and the mountains and the sky and suddenly I felt God very close to me. I knew I was joined completely with everything I saw. This was a moment I had no doubt about spiritual reality. I also remember that at the end of the Sunday drives our family used to take, I would pretend to be asleep and my father would carry me in his arms into the house. At those times, I saw clearly that he loved me. We are loved by God and loved by others. These are two basic truths that have returned to my awareness throughout my life. They are by no means obvious, nor was it clear to me at first that they are the same truth.

NOTHING NEED BE DONE
BEFORE WE ARE READY

My problems with God began early. As a child I had dyslexia and saw the word "God" as "dog." When I was sixteen, the Rabbi who had conducted my Bar Mitzvah confirmed me. Two months later he lost his faith and became a stockbroker. And then there was the time at the Cub Scout breakfast meeting when I ate a piece of bacon and God did not strike me down as He was supposed to. It would be an understatement to say that while I was growing up my faith in God waxed and waned.

At the Reformed Jewish Temple, I was taught that God could be kind and fair and that He would reward me for my good deeds, but punish me for wrong actions. I did not really think deeply about all of this until a close friend in high school was killed in an automobile accident. His death left me feeling not only depressed but angry and bitter as well. Where was God's fairness in all of this? "How can there be a just God," I asked myself, "if He would stand by and allow an innocent life to be snuffed out before it really had a chance to begin?" My answer was to turn from thinking of God altogether. If the question came up as to God's existence, I took the position of either an atheist or an agnostic.

Very quickly my judgments hardened against people who went to church or synagogue, or who turned to God in any way. I saw them as fearful and intellectually soft. A belief in eternal life seemed equally silly. I thought it was a concept that only people facing death would reach for, and that heaven was a fantasy for those who had made very little of themselves.

As I now look back, I think that without being completely aware of it, I was actually battling against what I thought were God's designs on my autonomy. I believed that I, Jerry Jampolsky, should be the sole director of my life. Only I could determine what was best for me and for the people in my life. I saw the will as an attribute of the mind and believed that each body held within it a separate mind. I believed that in order to fulfill my function in life, it was inevitable that I compete against other people's wills.

When I dared for a moment think there was a reality based on God's will, I was certain that it must be against me. If it operated unrestrained, it would surely prevent me from having the things that gave me pleasure. There were a few fleeting moments when I seemed to have a little willingness to let God be the director, but only as long as I thought there was a way to nudge Him to do things my way. Above all else, I wanted to remain in control and therefore the concept of God's will seemed very threatening.

As I mentioned earlier, what I conceived of as real was limited to the physical. And I thought that I, being only a small part of it, was very often a victim of the physical world. So this control that was so important to me was very limited indeed. Not once did it occur to me that God's will could be the part of me and everyone else that represents our deepest yearnings and most loving desires. Not once did I think that God's will and my true will were the same.

In most people's lives, no matter how strong their disbelief in God, there are brief moments when the darkness disappears and they experience peace and a joy that is not of this world. I remember one such incident when I was a third-year medical student. During that moment I *knew* there was a God. It was at night and I had just delivered my first baby on obstetrical service. The miracle of the perfection and harmony of what I experienced had to be greater than any one man's understanding. I was in awe: I felt there had to be a universal force, a miracle of love, beyond my comprehension. And I was part of that miracle, part of the whole. For that one moment, I saw that nothing in the universe was separate, that everything and everyone were joined.

Unfortunately, the feeling did not last long. That event became a cherished secret, and I went back to the books, tried to memorize, analyze, understand and make deductions based on a physical reality. And I became a non-believer in God again.

As far as prayer was concerned, I had no use for it. I thought that people who prayed were full of fear and were unrealistic. They were afraid to figure things out for themselves. I wanted nothing to do with such people. It was only much later that I realized I was the one who was fearful.

The late 1960's and early 70's found me with a successful private practice, some prestigious appointments and a growing national reputation in several fields. However, I had become a problem drinker, if not an alcoholic. In 1974, my marriage of twenty years ended in a painful divorce. I felt like a jigsaw puzzle that had been thrown into the air and scattered into a million pieces. I began sampling almost everything that came my way, both physical and mental. I tried all the therapies and all the groups, but nothing seemed to work. I knew I badly needed help, but I couldn't see any avenue open to me that offered even a glimmer of hope. I was aware that some people turned to God in their desperation, but that was not for me.

ALWAYS RESPOND WITH GENTLENESS

In 1975, I was still very much in this valley of depression, when one spring day a close friend and colleague called me long distance from a telephone booth and said she wanted me to read some unpublished material she had just received. It was a set of manuscripts entitled A *Course in Miracles*, and she said, she would bring them with her when she flew out to see me. In those days, I thought of this woman as the kind of person who becomes overly enthusiastic about too many things, but I loved her dearly, and so to placate her, I agreed.

The "course" she handed me was contained in black thesis

binders, and I began with a section that is now printed in pamphlet form under the title *Psychotherapy: Purpose, Process and Practice*. It was the best possible place for me to have begun. Anywhere else I would have been so put off by the heavy use of Christian terminology that I wouldn't have read further.

We ask for help and help is given. Often we do not recognize that other people's alcoholism, sexual betrayals, chronic illnesses, and alienating behavior are really cries for help. But unquestionably God recognizes every plea no matter what form it takes, and He finds some way to give us as much help as we are willing to receive at that time.

My help came in the form of A *Course in Miracles*, but I want you to know that I did not recognize it. At first, I was reading only to fulfill an obligation. As I continued, I was amazed at what happened. On a deep level that I did not even know existed in me, there was an instant in which I experienced the complete knowledge that I had found my path. Yet later I was shocked when I realized I had heard a voice within me saying, "Physician, heal thyself."

To my astonishment, I became totally immersed in the Course and found myself having periods of peace that I had not thought possible. A completely new life began to open up for me as I recognized that my purpose here on earth was only to experience God and to extend His peace. In other words, to teach only love. I then began to relate the Course philosophy to both my personal and professional lives and the artificial walls I had built up between the two started to dissolve.

It was in October of 1975, about five months after I began reading the Course, that a critical experience occurred. On a Sunday night I had gone out to dinner with some friends from Carmel. I had drunk a lot, but no more than usual, and I did not consider myself drunk. I went to bed about midnight, and around 2:00 A.M. I was awakened by a voice. For an instant I thought I was hallucinating and that in the next second I would begin seeing purple elephants on the wall and end up in delerium tremens. I was frightened and immediately sat up in bed. I heard it again. This time I knew it wasn't an external voice, but an internal one. Then it came for the third time: "You are entering a new phase of healing. It is no longer necessary for you to drink."

I started to sweat. What was I going to hear next? But I heard nothing more, and after about two hours, I finally got back to sleep. When I awoke in the morning, I had completely repressed the memory of what had happened. I shaved, showered and went off to work as usual.

I returned home about 6:30 P.M. and went into my customary routine of going straight for the Scotch bottle. However, as my hand began to reach for it, I heard the voice again: "This is a new phase of healing. It is no longer necessary for you to drink." My hand did not finish its journey. Surprisingly, in the days and months to come, I never missed drinking, never felt I was sacrificing, never thought I was being socially inadequate.

I believe that the purpose of God's guidance is to show us how to release our minds from fear so we may know His peace and be truly kind and sensitive to others, which we cannot do when we are fear dominated. Both "no" and "yes" must therefore be left to Love's guidance.

Within three months after hearing the voice, I lost thirty pounds, going from 192 to 162 pounds. Taking all my clothes to the tailor and having them taken in was a wonderful experience. It was as if I was confirming a miracle that part of me still doubted ever happened.

The Dr. Jekyll/Mr. Hyde existence I had led in which I had one personality in my office and another outside began to dissolve. It became apparent that the only way to find true peace was to live a unified life. Every aspect of myself had to be included.

Unless we see the importance of consistency in everything we think and say and do, our progress will be very slow. If our goal has not yet become to respond in gentleness to each call for help, we will also think that help is often withheld from us when we are crying out for it. Whenever we give help, we unfailingly see that the answer to all our needs is already within the very situation we think is hurting us. By becoming totally open and harmless, we see that there is no one who cannot help us and no instant when we are not surrounded by God's love and His guiding presence.

CHAPTER THREE

TEACH LOVE IN A FORM IT CAN BE UNDERSTOOD

The form of the teaching must be understandable to the student. A lesson that shows us a helpful approach to life can go unrecognized at first, but unless it is eventually recognized it is of no use to us. I'm sure that is one reason why the truth has come in so many different forms throughout the ages. There is someone to talk to everyone. If a book is needed, it appears. If it is a thought we need, or a moment of quiet, that is provided too. Each person we encounter and every event of our lives works together for our good, although we often don't see that at the time.

A *Course in Miracles* was the exact teaching aid I needed even though, as I have told you, I didn't recognize it as that at first. Since the principles of attitudinal healing are derived from this set of books, I would like to tell you about it and try to summarize some of the teaching it contains. I am not advocating them, for I believe you will find whatever aids to learning you need when you are ready for them. And I would like to remind you that when I was ready to give up drinking and, also, when I was ready for *A Course in Miracles*, Something in this universe did not let those opportunities slip by. In my case, I was literally *told* what to do. The events of your life *will* conspire to help you. You can trust that you will receive the help you need, when you need it, and in a form you personally can understand.

LOVE DOESN'T CARE
WHAT WE CALL IT

Coming from a Jewish background, I had difficulty with the Christian terminology used in the Course. This was especially true of Volume One, the *Text*. I would read a paragraph, and half an hour later, I would find myself still stuck on the same words. Eventually, I recognized that my inability to understand was due, in part, to my own resistance. I didn't *want* to understand words like "Christ," "Holy Spirit" and "salvation." It was as if my parents were looking over my shoulder saying, "No!" But, as I persisted, the meaning behind these terms gradually grew clearer, and I saw that the teaching of the Course was not the agitated, polarizing one I had seen on bumper stickers and billboards all my life.

When I first began to study the books, I would cover up the title and not tell anyone what I was reading. I didn't want to take the chance of having someone think I might be becoming a "spiritual nut" or a "Jesus freak." And I certainly didn't tell the people I was seeing in my office. So it was indeed quite a surprise that many of them began spontaneously to relate their spiritual experiences. This is an excellent example of how minds are always in communication. Apparently, I had given them unconscious permission to talk about these things, for they seemed to know that this was now acceptable. Before, I would have thought that their yearnings for God were completely irrelevant to their search for mental health.

I began to experience a major shift in how I viewed the people who came to me. I was now less likely to see them as having problems that I, because of my superior training and experience, was in a position to answer. Whatever I would have had to say to them before would have been for their ears, not for mine, and what they had to say to me would have been merely a clue to what they needed and not an indication of a problem we shared. I found that I was now beginning to listen to these people as teachers of great wisdom who had come to assist me. We could learn our mutual lesson much more quickly and easily together than apart, and that was the gentle reason we had been brought together.

I used to rely on Freud and other authorities for answers. Now I do my best to rely on God's inner voice for direction. I will pray, asking for guidance, with the people who come to see me, and I find that they work through their problems with greater speed and ease than they did before. The stress that I have been carrying around with me has lessened in this improved atmosphere of mutual acceptance and love.

Although I personally have found the Course to be an invaluable tool for assisting me on my own spiritual path, I do not think it would be helpful to everyone. I recommend it to some people; to others, I do not. But, as I said before, it is central to attitudinal healing, so I want to give you a very brief sketch of what it contains.

WHAT IS A COURSE IN MIRACLES?

The beauty of the Introduction from the Course speaks for itself:

This is a course in miracles. It is a required course. Only the time you take it is voluntary. Free will does not mean

that you can establish the curriculum. It means only that you can elect what you want to take at a given time. The course does not aim at teaching the meaning of love, for that is beyond what can be taught. It does aim, however, at removing the blocks to the awareness of love's presence, which is your natural inheritance. The opposite of love is fear, but what is all-encompassing can have no opposite.

This course can therefore be summed up very simply in this way:
> Nothing real can be threatened.
> Nothing unreal exists.

Herein lies the peace of God.

A *Course in Miracles* is a set of three books published by The Foundation for Inner Peace. It consists of a 622-page *Text*, a 478-page *Workbook for Students*, and an 88-page *Manual for Teachers*. It is self-taught and there is no organizational structure or leadership recommended or even implied within its teachings. The Foundation for Inner Peace does nothing but publish Course-related materials.

From studying these books I have come to see that there are only two emotions: love, our natural inheritance, and fear, an invention of our minds which is illusory. Each instant of the day we choose between these two, and our choice determines the kind of day we have and how we will perceive the world. If we teach fear, the description of reality that we will accept as our own will be full of fear. Yet a loving world will be ours when we extend only love. That means the world does not have to change before we can be happy, peaceful and thoughtful of others. *The only thing that has to change is our attitude.* A change in attitude is allowed, not forced.

Excitement began to build in me as I realized from my study of the Course that I possessed a wonderful potential: the capacity to change my perceptions. They could be corrected by choosing peacefully the thoughts I allowed myself to think. No longer was it necessary for me to see myself as crushed by circumstances. No longer need I blame other people for my unhappiness and stress. And, of course, I no longer had to demand that others change their perceptions. I only had to accept healing for myself. Perhaps nothing summarizes these ideas more succinctly than the following quote. It is also a perfect summary of attitudinal healing:

> **I am responsible for what I see.**
> **I choose the feelings I experience, and I decide upon the goal I would achieve.**
> **And everything that seems to happen to me I ask for, and receive as I have asked.**

The Course could be described as a form of spiritual psychotherapy. It implies that we are all therapists to each other, helping one another determine what is true and what is mere illusion. It teaches that we experience at-one-ment by seeing each other and ourselves as guiltless and by relinquishing fear. This helps us correct a fundamental error: the belief that anger brings us something we really want, and that, by justifying anger, we protect ourselves.

The Course views reality as composed only of God's thoughts, which are loving, constant and all-inclusive. It teaches that the real world, which reflects truth, can be viewed only through spiritual vision or love and not through the physical senses. Sin is defined as a lack of love. Evil, guilt and sin are recognized as misperceptions. In the illusory world, where we see only with our body's eyes, everything we behold has an opposite or a price, and nothing there is certain or constant or at rest. In the real world, we are at home, for we know God's love.

The Course emphasizes the acceptance of peace. It teaches its readers to concern themselves with the experience of God rather than with a gain in theological knowledge. It states that a *universal theology is impossible, but a universal experience is not only possible but necessary*. Although it uses Christian terminology, it stresses that the truth is all-inclusive. It states clearly that A *Course in Miracles* is only one of thousands of "courses" that can be utilized for personal transformation and salvation, and that each person will find his own way in his own time.

Salvation is such a fearful concept in some versions of Christianity that I would like to quote for you part of the answer, given in the third volume of the Course, to the question "How will the world end?"

> **The world will end in joy, because it is a place of sorrow. When joy has come, the purpose of the world has gone. The world will end in peace, because it is a place of war. When peace has come, what is the purpose of the world? The world will end in laughter, because it is a place of tears. Where there is laughter, who can longer weep? And only complete forgiveness brings all this to bless the world. In blessing it departs, for it will not end as it began.**

It is clear from this passage that the Course emphasizes forgiveness as both the short-term and long-term means for releasing our personal suffering and the plight of the world. We literally *see* our judgments. Because we judge, we perceive. And all perception, except what reflects love, presents to our mind the evidence that the laws and conditions of life are uncaring.

The Course is a teaching device that helps us to differentiate, and then to choose, between two thought systems, one of knowledge and one of perception. Knowledge is simply what is true. It is all that exists. What the mind perceives can be unreliable. We are still as Love created us, but we can see ourselves as something very unlike the creation of Love.

The thought system of perception is what we have all immersed our minds in, thinking it is real and defending its seeming reality to our very death. Yet it is merely a set of beliefs that makes the body both the focus and limit of our reality. By thinking of the body as our home, we picture birth as our beginning and death as the final summary of all we thought and did. There is no real hope of life beyond death because within this set of beliefs life and the body are perceived as one and the same.

This perceptual system is, of course, dependent on what we see and hear. Because we alone select all we choose to perceive, this system is both unstable and inaccurate. What we experience through our body seems to be real because it reflects what we *want* to see and hear. The Course states that **projection makes perception**. What we view as the world is merely an outpicturing of our inner thoughts and wishes. We disassociate ourselves from these images and deny that they started in our mind. We see the external world and the people in it as totally separate from ourselves, and we hide from our awareness the fact that all we see is a reflection of ourselves in a different form.

When we analyze our behavior, become self-critical and treat ourselves unkindly, we automatically make for ourselves a world that is angry, unloving and in despair. We then fail to realize that our only enemy is the attack thoughts we dwell on and the unloving attitudes we hold to. As we learn to recognize these mental errors, we can retrain our minds to look past them and see the world that reflects what God made. By letting go of all our distorted self-concepts, we can remember that the only thing real about us is love, which has always been here, the one Self that God created.

The guide out of the dilemma of two worlds is a mediator that goes by many names: Jesus, Guide, Teacher, the Voice of God, intuition, our higher self, our deeper self and countless other words and terms. This voice within is always present to help us when we call upon it and choose to listen to its message. Through forgiveness, it corrects the misperception that we are separate. In the instant of forgiveness, the illusory world of separation disappears and the real world of oneness and love is experienced. Life and the body are recognized as different rather than the same, and life is seen as eternal.

The Course gently encourages us not to make decisions by ourselves but to always seek the voice of peace within for guidance in all things. Our capacity to hear love's directions is an ability that most of us have not developed. However, we all have it. And it is only necessary that we begin. Each effort we make to follow our peaceful preference brings peace more fully into our experience. Developing our capacity to hear the leadings of love is essential to our progress because we will either consult fear or love in everything we do. There is no third alternative.

Before I started studying the Course, I almost always chose to listen to the counselings of conflict and fear rather than to my deep inner preference for peace. I used my mind as though its sole function was to be a fault-finder. The practical application of the Workbook lessons were most valuable to me as a way of retraining my mind, sharpening my capacity to listen and healing my attitudes toward others. For example, I had never before given any serious thought to the idea **I am not the victim of the world I see,** which is one of the 365 lessons contained in the Workbook. All my life I had sung the song: I *am* the victim of the world I see.

Other lessons I have found particularly helpful are:

> **I can elect to change all thoughts that hurt.**
> **I am never upset for the reason I think.**
> **Fear is not justified in any form.**
> **Only my condemnation injures me.**
> **Forgiveness is the key to happiness.**

These and the other lessons gave me a structured way to begin relinquishing the weighty investment in and attachment to the pain and guilt of my past. The way I looked at the world and the way I used my mind began to change. For the first time I started to understand the truth that to turn from judgments really is the key to happiness.

Although my resistance to this approach at times continues to occur, it does so with less frequency. However, I am still amazed, in spite of what I have said to you in this chapter, how often I prefer to be right rather than happy. Yet I am thankful that each moment is a new opportunity to choose peace instead of conflict and thereby to be more fully responsive to the needs of others.

This is what attitudinal healing is all about. It is the releasing of all thoughts from our minds except love thoughts. It is the correction of the misperception that we are separate from each other and that others are attacking us. It is relinquishing the need to analyze, interpret and evaluate our relationships. Attitudinal healing is simply seeing others as extending love or as being fearful and asking for our love. It is letting go of fear and guilt and choosing to see everyone, including ourselves, as innocent. Attitudinal healing occurs when we make the decision to teach only love.

CHAPTER FOUR

THE PRINCIPLES OF ATTITUDINAL HEALING

Shortly after I began working with A *Course in Miracles*, I felt guided to begin a center where children with life-threatening diseases could come and help each other in an atmosphere of freedom and acceptance. As a doctor, I had been trained to believe that controlled, predictable progress could only occur on a vertical plane. The patient was in no position to help himself because of his poor experience and limited knowledge. For him to attempt to assist other patients or to turn to them for help could be as dangerous as the blind leading the blind.

A *Course in Miracles* was now presenting me with another view, one that I had already begun to see through the type of insights I told you about earlier. This new view gave evidence of a different set of facts: That we have an internal physician, the voice of love. And that it can be heard when we recognize that it speaks not only in us but in the heart of everyone else, even the youngest child or the most unsophisticated and uneducated adults. We hear it by listening for it in others. Because it is love, it is in loving that we come to know it and trust it with every detail of our lives.

As a doctor, I had believed that gentleness and empathy were nice attributes to have, but that it was not absolutely necessary for the practice of love and the practice of medicine to go hand in hand. I came to see that healing and love are inseparable, and so I wanted our center to be a place where every attempt that anyone made to help himself or another would be thoroughly gentle and completely kind.

I envisioned not so much an organization as an atmosphere of mutual trust. Here, the doctors, therapists, volunteers and all the support people would come together with the children to learn from each other as equals, and not to "teach" from a position of superiority. At our center we have implemented this concept with a kind of dress code for all our groups and activities: Everyone must take off his M.D., Ph.D., R.N., M.S.W., or any other credential before entering.

I knew that the Center had to be a supplement to the traditional medical approach and not a substitute for it. The reason this point was so important was that the real choice we would be offering ourselves as well as the children would be one between conflict and peace. If as an organization we were to make the mistake of confronting the medical establishment we would be practicing the opposite of what we had set out to allow happen. The advice I still give to any parent who brings his child to me is, "Listen to everything your doctor tells you, but do not internalize what *anyone* tells you about the limits to your future chances. Because at this Center we *know* that your chances for freedom, happiness and peace are without any limit at all."

WE CAN BEGIN ONLY NOW

Those of us who joined together to start the Center shared the conviction that our real satisfaction and sense of accomplishment would come through our service to others. The wish to be of genuine help requires no long-range plans or dreams of expansion. We have worked hard to remain free of that kind of future orientation. Our interest was in broadening our perceptions and not in changing sick bodies into well bodies. Our central focus was to take an entirely new look at our own concepts of life and death and thereby to free our thought of fear.

I have noticed that a great deal of strife can result if people come together to pursue a purely external goal, even if the goal is very idealistic. They will attack each other whenever they perceive that another member of the group is standing in the way of the task that has been agreed upon. This they do in the name of a greater good. For example, they will think that another group member's feelings are not as important as the sick children they are all there to help. What is not realized is that only people with healed relationships are in a position to give the kind of help that will last. It is peace we want to extend, and to give peace we must first have it.

In 1975, a small group of us—Gloria Murray, Patsy Robinson, Pat Taylor and myself—met and formed The Center for Attitudinal Healing.* From the very start there has never been a charge for any service we have offered. We began with a few young children who had catastrophic illnesses such as cancer and muscular dystrophy, or with life-threatening conditions resulting from traumatic accidents. We soon discovered that the siblings and parents of the children felt a need for support from each other and so groups for them were also formed. Later we added groups for adults and young adults, and recently we have started a group for children whose parents have cancer.

Within the traditional model, the physician attempts to *do* something to the patient. Our goal at the Center is to be an educational model for self-learning. We administer no treatment. Since we are interested not in healing bodies but in healing minds, we define healing as the letting go of fear and health as inner

*The Center for Attitudinal Healing is presently located at 19 Main Street, Tiburon, California 94920.

peace. We join with the children with the mutual goal of freeing our minds of fear of ourselves, fear of relationships and fear of illness and death.

It is quite possible that the fear of death is behind every other terror we hold. I am certain it was this fear that was part of the reason I wanted to start the Center. Since children had always been my greatest teachers, I must have sensed that they would also be the ones from whom I would learn that even our ultimate fear is groundless. And indeed they teach this to all of us in a most beautiful way. When adults see these inwardly peaceful and joyous children on television, or standing before an auditorium of people, or in person at our Center, their fear of death subsides at least a little. I believe it is because before them is living proof that we can be happy and live lives that deeply benefit other people at the very time we appear to have some of the world's most dreaded illnesses and conditions. These children have taught me that our capacity to be happy and useful cannot truly be hampered by external conditions, even bodily ones, and that death will not frighten us if we decide to give to others from our internal treasure of love and peace.

Although my guidance was to have a place where the principles of *A Course in Miracles* would be demonstrated, it was also my guidance that the Course itself should not be taught, used or even recommended at the Center. Most of the people involved are not students of the Course, but they are in general agreement with the principles of attitudinal healing which are based on the Course. Although these principles have a universal spiritual base, the Center is not a religious organization, and the parents' or children's backgrounds or beliefs are of no concern to us. Anyone in a physical or emotional condition that one of our groups or projects deals with is wholly welcomed.

Here, then, are the principles of attitudinal healing:

THE SEVEN PRINCIPLES

1. **Health is inner peace.** *Therefore, healing is letting go of fear. To make changing the body our goal is to fail to recognize that our single goal is peace of mind.*

2. **The essence of our being is love.** *Love cannot be hindered by what is merely physical. Therefore, we believe the mind has no limits; nothing is impossible; and all disease is potentially reversible. And because love is eternal, death need not be viewed fearfully.*

3. **Giving is receiving.** *When our attention is on giving and joining with others, fear is removed and we accept healing for ourselves.*

4. **All minds are joined.** *Therefore, all healing is self-healing. Our inner peace will of itself pass to others once we accept it for ourselves.*

5. **Now is the only time there is.** *Pain, grief, depression, guilt and other forms of fear disappear when the mind is focused in loving peace on this instant.*

6. **Decisions are made by learning to listen to the preference for peace within us.** *There is no right or wrong behavior. The only meaningful choice is between fear and love.*

7. **Forgiveness is the way to true health and happiness.** *By not judging, we release the past and let go of our fears of the future. In so doing, we come to see that everyone is our teacher and that every circumstance is an opportunity for growth in happiness, peace and love.*

The use of these principles is, of course, not limited to children and adults with catastrophic illnesses. They have practical application for all of us. In the following chapters I will discuss each of the principles, give some examples of how they have been applied by others, and indicate how you can apply them in your life. But first, a little more about how we use them at the Center.

WE CAN ONLY HELP AN EQUAL

The group meetings start and end with everyone holding hands, closing his eyes, and experiencing joining and unity. We share problems and experiences and what we have found to be helpful, and as we do this we practice seeing each other as teacher. The emphasis is on equality regardless of age or background. This means the facilitators talk about their problems also.

As aids we sometimes use meditation, relaxation techniques, positive active imagination (mental imagery), art or prayer. We help each other with specific problems such as:

I'm embarrassed to go to school because I lost all my hair after chemotherapy.

I'm lonely and scared when I'm in the hospital.

Why did this happen to me?

I'm jealous of my brother because he gets all the attention because he's sick.

I'm afraid that my child is going to die.

My wife is withdrawing from me because I'm sick. I hate her for this and yet I love her and don't want to lose her.

We give our strength and support to each other by sharing similar feelings and how we handle them, but most of all by being nonjudgmental, defenseless, and by extending unconditional love.

In addition to the groups I have already mentioned, we also have a Pen Pal/Phone Pal program. An eight-year-old girl in Alaska with leukemia may keep in touch with another child her age in California who has already experienced what she is going through. Or a parent who has lost a child may help another parent with a gravely ill child. The Center pays for all long-distance calls.

There is also a program to train people who want to volunteer at the Center, incorporate our approach and philosophy into their own work, or start other centers. We provide educational outreach through the use of books, articles, audio and video tapes, and by participating in workshops, giving lectures at medical facilities and appearing on television shows. There has been a growing interest in our work, and many hospitals are now using our principles. Over twenty similar but autonomous centers have sprung up around the country, and more are beginning in other parts of the world.

Another program at the Center is one that is open to everyone, not just to those with catastrophic illnesses. We call it Person-to-Person. The Center serves as the catalytic agent for putting two people together who are given the simple instruction that their only aim is to be nonjudgmental and to practice forgiveness. The times and manner in which they wish to come together are left up to them.

When two people meet they often behave like insects bumping into each other. Their "antennae" begin flapping and they try to sense what about the other is different from them. They make comparisons and form quick judgments about each other's traits and appearance in order to decide whether they are dealing with a potential enemy or friend.

Usually we are only dimly aware of the activity of these "antennae," and yet we make automatic responses based on their limited and arbitrary comparisons to the past. We ignore the fact that this interferes with our seeing what is really happening now.

Consequently, we do not look at things freshly and take responsibility for changing our own thoughts.

In the Person-to-Person Program, it is suggested that we begin the encounter with an entirely different kind of mind set. We resolve beforehand that we will scan the other person for signs of love, gentleness and peace, and that the only information we will retain in our mind is that which will permit us to continue looking upon this person kindly. In other words, we seek only their innocence, not their guilt. We look at them with our heart, not with our preconceived notions.

This approach is one we all can use in our daily lives. We can start our own informal person-to-person programs, whether at work or in our more intimate relationships. We can form therapeutic partnerships in which each party agrees to offer unconditional support and love to the other.

I am frequently asked about how we manage financially, since all of our services are free. When I received the inner guidance to start the Center, I also heard, "Don't worry about money; just do the work and what money you need will be provided. Trust in God." The guidance also stated that I was to volunteer my own time, which I am still doing. Until recently, the staff consisted mainly of unpaid volunteers. As the Center has expanded, we have added some paid positions but still rely heavily on the many volunteers who so generously contribute their time.

For the first two years I paid the rent, phone bills and other overhead. Then a friend and benefactor, John Robinson, began to give us monthly financial support. As we became better known, we began to receive many contributions, from very small to larger ones. Later, we were awarded several large grants from foundations. As we expanded we began to create problems for ourselves, and at times had great difficulty in maintaining inner peace. We had many lessons to learn and are still learning.

Perhaps the best way to tell you about the Center is to discuss its principles in action. I will be doing that for the remainder of this book through the use of examples, many of which will be the stories of children with catastrophic illnesses. I have found these young people to be very powerful and inspirational teachers. If children with life-threatening diseases can attain inner peace, need we whose problems appear to be much less severe settle for a lesser goal?

CHAPTER FIVE

OUR GOAL IS PEACE

To have peace we have to recognize what there is in us already at peace. The place of peace is found within our mind. The body cannot tell us how to feel because the source of our experience is our mind and how we choose to use it. We are not a victim of the body and our mind cannot actually be threatened. For this reason there is always a way to freedom. That is why the first principle of attitudinal healing is:

Health is inner peace. *Therefore, healing is letting go of fear. To make changing the body our goal is to fail to recognize that our single goal is peace of mind.*

WE HAVE WHAT WE IDENTIFY

To have inner rest and contentment and an increasing experience of freedom and release, it is necessary for us to question our old sense of identity. Are we really only a body that lives a few moments and dies? Does the body set the limits to our strength, dictate how we must feel and define the tiny range of activities in which we can engage? Or is there a potential within us that knows no limit of any kind and is unending in its capacity to make happy and set free?

There is no point beyond which the combined power of the mind and will cannot go, because when united they allow thought to be flooded with love. Today there are many systems that are beginning to acknowledge that the body is not a limit on the mind, that there is a reality beyond what physical eyes can see and ears hear that awaits our recognition, and that a single Source unites all minds on a level that we can experience here and now.

There appears to be under way a philosophical and spiritual joining of East and West within these teachings. Organizations such as est, Actualizations, Silva Mind Control and a hundred others, although differing in particulars, all teach that the thoughts we hold determine our experience. They show their participants ways to change their perceptions of themselves and of the world. Attitudinal healing has a similar objective because once an individual begins to remove the barriers to his perception of love's presence within him, he has begun to heal himself on every level and in every way.

There are countless examples of people who, after serious illness or accidents, astound their doctors by their will to live, and undergo remarkable rehabilitation. Others, in spite of severe disabilities, lead happy, loving lives. This does not mean that our goal is physical healing or that if we do not heal our bodies we are wrong. Our goal is peace now—this very instant. It is central to our happiness that our years, long or short, be free of anger and that our body be used as a means of giving others the gift of kindness.

Each of us, to experience peace, must recognize that we have a choice as to whether we view our identity as small and severely limited or as unlimited as love. We do not have to set any boundaries on our health or happiness because our doctor, parents, friends, the media or society may have told us that there will always be things we cannot change. The attitudinal healer does not counsel adjustment to pain and death or compromise with misery, because it is possible for anyone to quietly listen to his inner guide, who will teach him the way to freedom. Love knows no place it cannot go and no person it cannot bring rest.

WITHIN GOOD THERE IS NO LIMIT

We spend a great deal of time at the Center reminding each other that nothing is impossible. Tinman Walker has been, and continues to be, a very effective teacher of this concept. He is now twenty-two years old. When he was fourteen he collided with a truck while riding his bike down a hill. Due to the severity of his injuries, there was little hope for his survival. After a subdural hematoma (a mass of blood under the covering of the brain) was removed, he remained in a coma. The medical team caring for him held little hope for his regaining consciousness, and if he did, they said he would be a vegetable. When he was sent home, still comatose, the family was advised to put him in an institution. However, believing in the healing power of love, they had other ideas for his care.

Eighty-one days after his accident, Tinman awakened. He had a spastic paralysis on the right side of his body and his speech was labored and difficult to understand. He was given the best physical and occupational therapy his parents could find, and, in time, he was able to return to school.

Prior to his accident Tinman had been an outstanding athlete, but now he was barely able to walk. Because of his physical handicaps, he saw himself as a social outcast. Much of his time was spent at home, friendless and alone.

At the end of three and a half years, a speech therapist who was evaluating him said that Tinman had made about all the progress he was going to make. He and his family became discouraged and decided to seek help from our Center, because they had heard that we believed nothing was impossible.

When Tinman first came to us, he was severely limited in many ways. His speech was slow and halting. Because of the degree of paralysis which still remained, he walked very deliberately and with a limp. But what impressed me most about him when we first met was the sparkle in his eye. Immediately, I had a strong feeling he and I were going to be significant teachers to each other and that miracles were to be expected in our lives.

A week after we met, I was given two theater tickets and I asked him to join me. He agreed. But first we went to a restaurant, where he had considerable trouble eating. It not only took him a long time to finish dinner, but after we left, he had difficulty walking up the San Francisco streets. I could see what a great teacher of patience he was going to be to me and must already have been to his family.

Tinman spent a lot of time with the group at the Center and much one-to-one time with me. He also found a good physical therapist who was willing to work with him. We all had one goal. We were determined to see that Tinman turn out to be much more than a negative statistic. And when two or more minds join to achieve a single loving goal—watch out!

We began to make open loop tapes that he could play to himself during his sleep. At first, only my voice was on them but later he used his own. "Open loop" tapes are casette tapes designed to repeat continuously a 3-to-5 minute recording. They are simple to use and widely available.

On the initial tape, I suggested to Tinman that he view his brain as a blackboard and erase from it any memory of a time he had difficulty with his speech. In place of these scenes of distress, I instructed him to picture scenes in which a steady improvement in his speech pattern occurred. Similar suggestions were made regarding his walking problems, his spastic paralysis and other related problems. Every night negative pictures were erased mentally and replaced by positive pictures of his functioning more freely. These mental pictures were to be visualized in specific form, such as seeing himself skiing and driving a car.

About a month later, Tinman came to my office and asked me to watch him. He said he was going to put a hole right where he was standing. With glee, he jumped about six inches off the floor and landed still standing. It was the first time he could do this since his accident.

The other young people in Tinman's group at the Center were very patient with him. He liked to tell jokes and, to most of us, it seemed that he took forever to finish a story. Later, he told me that the Center had been the first place where people were patient enough to listen to his stories without interrupting or trying to finish his sentences for him. As we go through the day, we often become anxious to save time. But what better use of our time is there than to listen to another in love?

After Tinman's speech had improved, he found another use for positive mental imagery. At one meeting, he told us he was having a tough time with Italian at school. Every time he took an oral exam, he froze up and was unable to give the correct answer. I suggested that he close his eyes and think of himself in a place where he would be relaxed. For Tinman, this was in the mountains. I then had him erase all the old tapes in his mind of when he had done poorly on examinations and replace them with positive tapes showing himself as calm, relaxed and answering test questions correctly. I also suggested that he view his teacher as a friend trying to help him rather than as an enemy trying to find his weaknesses and embarrass him. I said that until the next test he should practice this imagery each morning on awakening and just before he went to sleep at night. If he became fearful while doing his imagery, he was to pause and visualize himself as relaxed in the mountains. He was then to proceed with this "positive active imagination" until he could do it five times in a row without experiencing fear.

At the next meeting, Tinman excitedly told us of his great success on the Italian test. Other kids in the group admitted they were also having troubles with tests, so he became a teacher to them, again proving the far-reaching influence of a positive belief system.

Possibly the high point in my work with Tinman was an event that drew tears of happiness to my eyes. I was going to give a lecture to a group of physicians in Los Angeles and asked him to join me. He replied, with a smile on his face, that he wouldn't be able to because he was going cross-country skiing.

WE ARE NOT A BODY.
WE ARE FREE.

Joe Marks is another example of a child going beyond the seeming limitations of his body, beyond what was thought even remotely possible. I'm going to let his mother, Mary Marks, tell you part of Joe's story.

Working one night in September of 1977, in southern California, where I was studying at a chiropractic college, I received a phone call informing me that my two boys, who were living with their father and stepmother in northern California, had been in an accident with a tractor. The younger one was unhurt, but they thought

I should get up there because they didn't know if the older boy was going to pull through.

No planes were flying directly from Los Angeles to Eureka, so it took me fifteen hours to arrive at the hospital. I found my twelve-and-a-half-year-old lying in the critical care unit naked under a sheet with a huge bandage on his head, his leg in traction, several intravenous bottles dripping into him and various tubes, including two in his nose, one for oxygen and the other pumping his stomach. It was an incredible sight and not the boy I had seen a few weeks before who was a normal, healthy preteenager. The accident had left him with broken ribs, three fractures of the pelvis, his right thigh broken in half, multiple skull fractures—the whole base of his skull was in little pieces—and spinal fluid leaking from his ear. His head looked like a crushed watermelon. He was not expected to live very long.

Without going into any more gory details, I can say that so many of his functions were impaired he couldn't breathe, and among other complications, he had developed pneumonia. The EEG brain wave tests showed nothing but slow, rolling waves—almost flat— indicating that if Joe, by some miracle, did live, he would obviously be a vegetable, unable to move or think. As for the rest of him, there wasn't much to do for broken ribs and, at first, they just held his leg in traction without setting it; later, they used pins and a cast so that he could be moved more easily.

We stayed with Joe twenty-four hours a day. There wasn't much else we could do for him. Yet recently, when someone suggested that I visualize a beautiful place, my thoughts went to that intensive care ward and sitting next to Joe. There was nothing left of that boy but pure love. He seemed blank, not to be participating at all. His eyes never moved and even though his fingers were pinched, his nervous system was so depressed there wasn't even a primitive response. And he lay there like that for three months, yet for me it was a joy just to be there with him. It seemed like the whole state of California knew that Joe had been hurt. There were constant prayers for him and a regular meditation at nine o'clock every evening. The whole room seemed to light up, and Joe would seem to glow just lying there without giving any response. People would come in just to be with him, and often comment on a kind of love or energy they felt being there. That, of course, reinforced my own ability to express love to him.

After about five weeks it was recommended that he be institutionalized, but we didn't accept that. So we made arrangements to take him to a hospital on an Indian reservation near where his father and his family lived. It was a very small place with just nine beds supervised by a physician who had been a good friend of the family.

Suddenly, I found I had a lot of input into Joe's life. The doctor was very interested in nutrition and asked me to govern Joe's diet. He had been getting a sort of milk shake through the tube in his nose. I changed the formula to include a lot of ground-up vitamins and minerals; I made him a bunch of brightly colored gowns to replace the white ones he wore; I washed him, brushed his teeth for him and combed the little bit of hair that was growing back. We played rock and roll and classical music in his room all the time, and sitting there in that room became my home, my whole existence.

I spent a lot of time holding and stroking Joe. Then we'd move his arms and legs and turn him to avoid bedsores. He was supposed to have the bed cranked up for better circulation, but instead I would hold him upright and hug him a lot. Of course, he was completely out of it; but he was my kid; I loved him and it didn't matter that the only response I got was the warmth of his body.

Then even that little hospital was saying there was no justification for his being there any longer. He had improved in many ways. The pneumonia was gone, as was the kidney infection and catheter. The tracheotomy tube had been removed; the scars were healing; the bones mending. He was ticking away, but not awake. He was in a coma, and they wanted us to take him somewhere else.

But just before the Marks family had to take Joe out of the hospital, he began to respond: first by squeezing his father's hand; later, by moving a leg upon his mother's request. Not only could he hear her voice, despite the fact his ear drums had been punctured and all the bones shattered, but he was following commands.

When Mary Marks heard about her son that first September night, her immediate reaction was anger. The feeling lasted only a few moments before her attitudes and feelings began to shift.

I started a mental dialogue with Joe, telling him that I understood, that everything was okay, that if his spirit needed to leave, it was all right. Either way, I told him mentally, would be fine. I didn't really pray for his healing as much as I constantly prayed for understanding of what had happened.

It is most difficult to convey to you the devotion, the acceptance, the love that his father, Keith, his stepmother, Sharon, and his mother, Mary, showered on Joe. They all felt that Joe was a part of the family, no matter what shape he was in, and they fully intended that he should experience this sense of belonging at all times.

It was after the end of his stay at the Hoopa hospital that Joe's grandmother mentioned my name to Mary. She was a student of *A Course in Miracles* and had heard me lecture about the mind being limitless. She had also been impressed with the story of Tinman Walker. Joe's doctor phoned and asked me to consult on the case. I flew to Eureka where he was going to meet me and fly us to the small town of Hoopa. However, there was a storm which prevented any further air travel, so we ended up driving.

We finally found the trailer that Joe and his mother were living in. Joe was lying in bed looking extremely sad. He was not able to talk and was completely blind with bilateral optic atrophy. He was almost completely paralyzed. In spite of all of this, I felt that spirit of positive expectation, the "We can" attitude coming from Joe, his mother and even the very atmosphere within that small trailer.

I explained to Joe and his mother about our work at the Center and related the story of Tinman and other youngsters we have seen. I emphasized our belief that minds are joined and that nothing is impossible, and I told them about a project of ours headed by Tammy Cohen, and, later, Cheryl Balsan, in which we were teaching blind children to sense color and objects without touching them. I mentioned to Joe that there was a fourteen-year-old blind boy named Harold Alexander who could not only identify colors but also ride his bicycle and do many other things that most people wouldn't have expected. Joe became intrigued with these possibilities.

For the next hour, we experienced together some aspects of the fact that all minds are joined. I would send Joe the thoughts, "red" or "blue." He would nod his head vertically for red, horizontally for blue. Within the hour, he was 80% accurate in identifying the right colors and his depression began to disappear. He even became quite animated.

I told Joe that his mind was not limited to his body, and I shared with him this lesson from the Course:

I am not a body. I am free. For I am still as God created me.

I also suggested three other things to him. First, that he could put thoughts of motion pictures in his mind in which he would see himself walking and talking. Second, that since he still had faith in God, he could join with God, erase all doubts and accept that in God nothing is impossible. Third, since in a few days he was going to fly to Los Angeles to enter a special rehabilitation hospital for the neurologically damaged, I suggested that although he might not feel anyone in the world could be worse off than he was, when he got to the hospital it would be beneficial for him to find someone else he could help.

About a month later, I received a letter from Mary. She told me that Joe had been experiencing periods of deep sadness. On his ward, there was a small child who was suffering from an irritation to the central nervous system and was crying all the time. No drug seemed to help. Mary remembered what I had said about Joe's helping someone, and all of a sudden she found herself picking up this small child and carrying him over to Joe's bed. She plopped him onto his lap.

At first, Joe looked startled. Then, with his left hand, which had a little movement in it, he began to gently stroke the child, who stopped crying almost immediately. Mary described the situation as if both children had risen to a higher state of consciousness where there was just bliss and peace.

I flew to Southern California several times to visit Joe and his family. On one visit, I took Tinman Walker with me. The timing was perfect. Joe, his stepmother and mother were getting discouraged. Tinman walked in and began telling Joe that he was doing things the doctors never thought possible and that Joe could do them also. "You just have to keep saying, 'I can; nothing is impossible,' and keep getting rid of all your doubts." Later, Joe's family said that seeing Tinman was worth more than what anyone else had said to them or anything they had read. It was the first time they had actually seen someone who had been in a state similar to Joe's who had truly made it. A couple of months later, with some assistance, Joe began to walk.

Later I went to Fullerton, California, with members of our staff and some of our children to make a presentation at a conference. I phoned Mary the night before to see how things were going. She was exuberant. Joe had started talking! I asked if they would be interested in coming to the conference and participating; her response was an ecstatic "Yes!"

On the day of the conference, the auditorium was filled with health professionals. When it was Joe's turn to speak, he got up and said, "You never know for sure what another person can do in the future. Look at me. I was supposed to be a vegetable. Tell your patients never to give up, that nothing is impossible—just look at me." Tears came to my eyes and I think to everyone else's as well.

On another occasion I took Harold Alexander, who was blind, and his girlfriend to see Joe. That weekend was an experience I will never forget. Can you imagine how I felt after we got on the plane and discovered that Harold had never flown before? To be able to share a blind person's first experience on an airplane was a gift indeed!

When we got to Joe's house, Harold began to tell him how the previous week his sister and her girlfriend had come to his house. When they entered the room, he said to the girlfriend, "There's something different about your clothes today." She said, "How can you know? You're blind." He started to give us his reply when Joe interrupted and said, "I know what you saw; she wasn't wearing a bra." Whereupon Harold, looking very surprised, said, "How did you know? You weren't there." Then they both broke into laughter. Here were two boys who had on different occasions experienced being able to sense when a girl was not wearing a bra, even though they couldn't see her, and now they were witnessing to each other the possibilities of the mind.

That day I saw Harold's girlfriend taking pictures of him. Later on, as I was talking to Keith, Joe's father, I looked up and couldn't believe my eyes. There was Harold holding a camera and taking a picture of his girlfriend! (By the way, the picture turned out great.) Shortly after our visit, Joe began taking pictures also, centering the subjects with remarkable accuracy.

Joe is now living in Idaho with his father and stepmother. He walks without any support, is a good swimmer and attends regular high school classes at his age level. He continues to make progress and to be a light and teacher to us all.

FEAR IS AN INVITATION TO PEACE

I am very thankful for the time I spend with these young teachers because they are continually reminding me there are no boundaries we cannot step beyond—a concept I keep mentioning, yet somehow keep forgetting. I don't see how it would be possible for anyone to know Tinman, Joe or Harold without seeing the part that the relinquishment of fear plays in healing.

When viewed correctly, fear can be reinterpreted as our mind's invitation for us to rise to a higher level of freedom. We are not being called to run away from danger, but toward safety. And there is a world of difference between these two directions.

Safety lies in "We can." We always choose between that which affirms life and what merely denies it. Either our thoughts support and lift us upward or they begin sinking us into depression and hopelessness. Even the least of our criticisms or complaints supports an entire belief system that denies the light within each living thing before us. Our ideas are like the stones of a path we travel. There is not a single thought that does not take us somewhere. That is why we must not leave our mind in conflict if we wish to walk toward health and peace.

To be free of conflict requires only one thing: a goal that is not itself conflicted. Trying to change anything is a form of battle; wanting something that can only be ours in the future is to block our potential to be happy now. Therefore, set for yourself a goal that can be fulfilled where you stand. Make this instant your door to freedom and you will find that it will crack open a little further each time you return to this moment in peace.

CHAPTER SIX

WE ARE LOVE

The principles of attitudinal healing are interdependent and interrelated. As I continue to discuss them and give examples, you will see that they overlap and that each discussion and example generally includes aspects of other principles. The second principle of attitudinal healing is:

> **The essence of our being is love.** *Love cannot be hindered by what is merely physical. Therefore, we believe the mind has no limits; nothing is impossible; and all disease is potentially reversible. And because love is eternal, death need not be viewed fearfully.*

Love is the part of us that is real. Because love itself is our potential, we are not limited by the body and are not subject to any of the body's conditions or "laws." Communication with others is from love to love and not from our past experiences to theirs. No two past experiences are identical and communication that rests on judgments is inherently conflicted. Yet when communication is based on love, it is deeply satisfying and healing. Even our fear that death could interrupt it begins to vanish.

What, then, is love? Because it must be experienced in order to be meaningful, I can't define it for you except to say that it is the total absence of fear and the recognition of complete union with all life. We love another when we see that our interests are not separate from his, and so we join with him in what he truly wants. This is a union of the higher minds and not an alliance of egos.

It isn't possible to evaluate or prove love in the usual ways. The fact that we are not able to measure it does not make it any less real. We have all had glimpses of pure, unconditional love, and there is unquestionably a part of us that knows it exists. We start to become aware of love whenever we choose to accept people without judging them and commence the gentle effort of giving without any thought of getting something in payment. This means, for example, that true love is not giving in order to change another's attitude from a bad mood to one of lightheartedness or from ingratitude to one of thanks to us. True love is a completely pure and unencumbered form of giving. It is extended freely to the love in others and is its own reward.

The word love, as we generally use it, means something quite different from real love. It is giving in order to get. It is a bargain, a trade arrangement. This is often fairly obvious in romantic relationships in which each partner is giving with the expectation that it will be returned in the specific form that is desired. Conditional love is also what passes for kindness in most parent/child relationships. Here, the extension of love is contingent on approved behavior and attitudes. Parents frequently seek an affirmation of their own worth through the accomplishments of their child and through payments of respect. A child often loves his parents only when he gets what he thinks he wants, whether this be a new possession or approval and praise. Such love is not dependable or permanent; its temporary nature causes us to carry an underlying fear that we are about to be abandoned.

When we are giving actual love, our concern is not with our own or anyone else's behavior. We feel natural because we recognize that love is our natural state. We are not aware of limits. We don't question the possibility of anything good and we are not preoccupied with time. We are conscious of now and all it contains. When we are extending love, we are free and at peace. Attitudinal healing shows us how to allow ourselves to experience this kind of love, the only love there is.

LOVE IS OUR ESSENCE

We all believe that we want to have less conflict, fear, stress and depression. And deep within our heart we do desire this. But on the level from which we function most of the time, we do not choose peace over conflict and happiness over fear because of the sacrifices we believe this choice would entail. We actually think that we can get satisfaction from revenge. That we can be right by proving someone else wrong. That to humble someone who is being difficult will gain for ourselves "a little peace and quiet." It seems logical to us to be stern with our children in order to teach them gentleness. We think there are people who deserve to lose because of their behavior and that justice is the pain they receive. We try to increase love with one person by excluding others. We believe that guilt is attraction. That pain can be pleasurable. That taking is gaining. But we are puzzled as to why this approach to life does not give us peace and yet we can see no reason to change our basic beliefs.

It is clear that we need an experience that will bring sanity to our mind. The experience we all need more of is love. In order to move more deeply into the atmosphere of love, we have to begin identifying less with the body and more with our love-related emotions because these feelings speak to us of that which has always been within us but what our shabby self-image has not allowed us to see. To see it we have to bring it forth, for only by extending what is good will we know that the good is within us and that we ourselves are good. However, to bring it out does not always mean to act it out, but rather to bring it into our hearts and minds.

A preoccupation with the body and its behavior will not allow love to flood our mood because the body is merely what is different. To love, we have to recognize what is the same about us and all living things. The love in us can unite with the love in others, but two bodies cannot become one.

All emotions that center on the body to the exclusion of others are negative or self-denying. As a first step, we must honestly and *gently* question our investment in how our body looks, with how we have adorned it, honored it, employed it and with whether we are receiving a fair amount of credit, thanks, influence, money or popularity for what our body has done. Because, in proportion as we value a body identification, we tend to downplay or ignore altogether our essense, love.

The gentle questioning of our low self-image does not call for vast changes in behavior or life style. It calls for nothing more than an honest looking around and a simple, calm noticing, especially an inner noticing. Once true value is recognized, if any external changes are needed, these will occur by themselves and in their own time. If we become preoccupied with what we do rather than how we do it, we always needlessly delay ourselves. Attitudinal healing is concerned only with how. Are we acting *with* love, *with* peace, *with* happiness and *with* certainty? For if we are, whatever we do will be right.

A preoccupation with other people's bodies and bodily behavior leads us to believe that our body determines what kind of person we are and what kind of relationships we must settle for. We may get momentary pleasure from the fact that others seem less attractive than we do, and some people may be drawn to us because of our personality or special accomplishments, but we always know in our hearts that relationships based on such feelings are shallow and fleeting. We really don't want people to be attracted to us because of our bodies but because of what there is about us that will not change. We want people to understand us and love us because they understand us. This they cannot do while relating to us only as a body. We want to be aware, and we want others to be aware, of the golden glow from within and not merely the glitter of surface appearances. And we determine this outcome by what we ourselves identify with. What we put forth, mentally and emotionally, is what is related to by others. We are either extending gentleness, joy, kindness, openness and peace or we are hiding behind a purely physical identification. We can't do both because one is love and the other is fear.

NOTHING REAL IS IMPOSSIBLE

This concept was life changing for Colleen Mulvihill, a twenty-three-year-old woman who was a senior working toward a Movement Education degree at a liberal arts college in northern California. Colleen was pretty enough to model, and she sometimes did. When I first met her, she also had two, year-round, part-time jobs, one as a sports medicine coordinator in her college athletic department and the other as a tutor in the school's developmental movement laboratory where children with neurological and academic handicaps are helped to develop motor skills. During the summer months, she had assumed an additional job of teaching swimming and crafts at a nearby day camp. Colleen lived in a small apartment 500 miles away from her family, and her best friend was a German shepherd named Sasha, a Seeing Eye dog.

When she first came to me, Colleen was legally blind. (The term applies to those whose sight is so limited that they cannot function as sighted, although they might have a small amount of close vision.) From birth, she has had a condition known as rentrolental fibroplasia, which is a progressive accumulation of scar tissue behind the retina which may eventually cause blindness or at least severely limited vision.

When she was born, it was standard medical practice to put

premature infants into high-pressure oxygen tanks. Later in life she was told that it was such a procedure that had caused her blindness. Possibly you can imagine the rage and resentment a person with this condition might have against the world. Colleen indeed had such feelings as well as a great deal of pain that is often associated with this type of disease.

She was born and raised in the Los Angeles area by parents who saw value in her attending regular public school instead of special schools for the handicapped. They reasoned that this would better prepare her for the real world. It was obviously a good decision for Colleen, although there is, of course, no right or wrong procedure that can be applied to all cases involving handicapped children. With the understanding assistance of teachers who always seated her in the front of the room and gave her additional auditory and visual cues, she graduated from both elementary and high school and then decided on a small college away from home.

This intelligent and highly spirited girl found her situation more difficult as her limited vision continued to fade. In 1975, Sasha, a two-year-old Seeing Eye dog, came into Colleen's life. She and Sasha trained together in North Hollywood and have been inseparable companions ever since. Sasha accompanied her to college classes and even to the State Capitol in Sacramento where Colleen was an active lobbyist for the National Federation of the Blind.

Several years ago, Colleen became aware that many people were discussing supplements to traditional medical procedures and she began to hear evidence that the mind can affect the body. It was shortly after this that she began to visit me. I introduced her to *A Course in Miracles*.

Later, I referred her to the adult attitudinal healing group at our Center. I emphasized to her that the mind knows no boundaries and that nothing is impossible. I told her to let go of every negative value she ever had, to not limit herself to her past beliefs or confine herself to a reality that came to her only through her physical senses.

We talked about the very important concept from A *Course in Miracles*:

There is no order of difficulty in miracles.

Miracles can be defined as shifts in perception which remove the blocks to our awareness of love's presence. Therefore, they can be seen as a natural occurrence. Although miracles are not physical phenomena, changes at the physical level may sometimes accompany them. I shared with Colleen my conviction that anyone can learn to shift his perception and see the presence of love and that this is true sight.

One day, Colleen asked a question that was very important to her. "Is it possible for me to regain my sight?" I replied, "Anything is possible. You do not *have* to be a negative statistic on a probability curve of people with rentrolental fibroplasia."

She began to grasp the idea that the thoughts we put into our minds determine our perceptions. She began to work on "positive mental pictures," and to activate the principles in A *Course in Miracles*. Practicing peace of mind, peace of God, became her single goal; practicing forgiveness her single function; and listening to, and being directed by, her inner voice became her way of experiencing a sense of completion and oneness. She began to forgive God and the universe for her blindness. Her bitterness dissolved and was replaced by an increasing sense of peace. As this happened, her head and neck pains began to ease.

Gradually, a subtle but quite real change began to take place in the way Colleen pictured herself. She told me later, "It was as though my attitude about myself began to shift. Where I had always treated myself as a blind person, I now began to think of myself as normal." Even so, Colleen was totally unprepared for the partial recovery that happened in March 1978. Her daytime vision improved enough so that she could see where she was going, and her ophthalmologist informed her that she was now legally sighted during the daytime although she remained legally blind at night. When I talked to him on the phone, he stated that he had never seen a person with Colleen's condition make this kind of visual improvement.

Her increasing ability to see brought a new set of problems involving Sasha. "It is, very traumatic," Colleen explained, "for a guide dog to find she is not essential for the totality of her master's mobility." But that problem, too, was gradually solved as she and Sasha worked together for a new understanding of each other's needs.

Colleen continued in school to prepare herself to be of service to others who are ill. She is primarily interested in the holistic health approach in which one attempts to assist the whole person rather than to treat only sick organs. She has helped many people at our Center and in other cities and has been active in our telephone network, working with blind people on the phone throughout the United States.

Recently, Colleen called me. "Jerry," she said, "I want to take you for a drive." "What do you mean?" I said. "I am now licensed to drive a car in two different states and am legally sighted for both day and night." I want you to know, my drive with Colleen Mulvihill was the happiest time I have ever had in a car, even though I cried.

There are many times I forget some of the principles I have mentioned in this book and I end up depressed. When I see Colleen and experience her unconditional love, I am aware that she also sees the light in me, and this helps me let go of feelings of darkness by reminding me of my true reality. To me, Colleen brings to life Jesus' statement as it appears in a modern translation: "I have come into the world to give sight to those who are spiritually blind and to show those who think that they see that they are blind."

Judgment is blind. Only love sees.

LOVE IS ETERNAL

It is clear we will not be at peace as long as we think of ourselves as vulnerable to sickness and accident, growing old, becoming feeble and dying. Without a change in perception about what we are, anxiety will continue to underlie all we think and do as we anticipate the approach of our final annihilation. Somehow we must begin to recognize that we live now and eternally as love. I believe we are in this world only to learn and teach love. The lengths of our assignments vary, but what each of us gives and is given is the same: love.

Working with children facing death, and also with their families, has helped me begin to overcome my own fear of death and to question the belief that death is final. You might wonder how the Center staff can work intimately with these youngsters, watch some of them die, and yet not destroy ourselves emotionally. Speaking for myself, I could not continue if I still held to the belief that death is the end of life. If I really thought that, these children's deaths would indeed tear me up too much to go on.

Most of us at the Center try to look at death as a transition. We feel blessed to know these youngsters and their families. They teach us that there is a difference between life and the body, that the body is temporary but life, being spirit, is unending. Their message has been one of life, eternal life and that living is synonymous with loving.

The first of the Center's children to die was Greg Harrison. He was eleven years old. When there were no more new drugs to be administered and it appeared he didn't have much more time left, Greg was asked by the other children in his group, "What do you think it will be like to die?" I know I will never forget his answer. He said, "I think that when you die, you just discard your body, which was never real in the first place. Then you are in heaven, at one with all souls. And sometimes you come back to earth and act as a guardian angel to somebody. I think that's what I would like to do." Greg's attitude toward death shows that any occurrence in this world *can* be looked at with love. And it is, of course, such a relief to ourselves and others to do so.

Another member of our Center family, Will Stein, a fourteen-year-old with Ewing's sarcoma, taped an interview with me two weeks before he died. It was his belief that we all agree to certain assignments before being born into this world. Some are for long periods, others are shorter, but the length of time doesn't matter. Will felt his assignment was a short one but that while he was still breathing, his assignment was not over.

As long as our bodies are alive, our job is to use them as a means of allowing our love to extend in a form that others can recognize and receive. Because of the basic gentleness of their spirits, many children will demonstrate how love can be extended even when they are not in a physical position to do good deeds. It is what we all do with our hearts that affects others most deeply. It is not the movements of our body or the words within our mind that transmit love. We love from heart to heart.

There is, of course, no rule as to how a loved one is to be remembered. And the *appearance* of peace and joy should never be forced. However, during the course of a child's illness, some parents come to the realization that their child is more than a body, and they then know that their relationship with him will not end with his death. I am convinced this is not deception but the recognition of reality. When death occurs, it makes what these parents feel after their child has gone not only bearable but peaceful because they continue to feel a joining with their child through love.

The attitude of Bryan Bradshaw's family following his death is an illustration of an emphasis on spiritual reality rather than on bodies. Bryan was an eight-year-old who had one leg amputated as a result of bone cancer. His courage was remarkable, and he and his family were strong teachers to us all.

About a week before Bryan died, I visited the family in San

Jose and spent some time with his six-year-old sister, Lorrie Ann. I asked her to draw a picture about what was going on in her mind. It showed Bryan with wings on his sides going up to heaven. She said, "When you are in heaven there is no sickness or pain. You are just happy and feel love because you talk to God all the time."

One of our staff members and I went to San Jose to be with Bryan's family the day he died. We were impressed with their sense of peace. We saw that many tearful friends who came to their home were helped by their calming influence. Some of the children who were there felt guilty because they had not visited Bryan as much as they thought they should have. They, along with Bryan's parents, went with us to the family room to talk things out. After awhile, the children's guilt lessened, and they began to tell stories of funny times they had had with Bryan. Whenever we lose interest in guilt, only love, remains.

Since Bryan's family had no religious preference, they asked Tom Pinkson, a friend from the Center, and me to conduct a memorial service that would allow those attending to leave feeling happier than when they came. I began my remarks by sharing Lorrie Ann's picture and her comments about it. Tom talked about the many ways in which Bryan and his family had helped others. And we both told about the feelings we had experienced in Bryan's presence and the beauty and love we were feeling that day. Then the entire group joined in singing some of Bryan's favorite songs. We were led by Rabbi Nathan Segal, who had become friends with Bryan at a Center picnic.

Following the service, helium balloons were given to everyone. Bryan loved balloons. At one moment, we released 100 of them, along with our individual messages of love to Bryan and the universe. The balloons appeared to join together in a rainbow and float into the sky. Several parents came up and said how much they had dreaded bringing their children to the memorial service, but how surprised and relieved they were to experience happiness rather than grief on such an occasion.

WE NEED FEAR NOTHING

Those, of course, are not the only children from our Center who have died. I have mentioned these few because each of them has personally taught me a lesson strongly related to the words *death need not be viewed fearfully*. A fearful perception is of no use to anyone. And my work at the Center has shown me how genuinely helpful it is for us to look at all things in peace. It is only a gentle vision that allows us to see that what we are—and all that we are—is pure love.

Not long ago the Center had an all-day meeting for about twenty-five families who had each lost a child. Many of these children had not attended our groups but the comments and stories related by their parents reminded me of the inner core that unites every person on this earth. We are all members of a single family and each person is our brother, even though we often forget this.

A number of the parents at this meeting said that even while he was dying their child had been their teacher and that in many respects the traditional roles of parent and child had been reversed. And all of the parents stated that the loving spirit of their child seemed to continue as a strong and comforting presence in their heart and that in many ways they felt a continuation of the actual relationship. This, they said, was a very healing experience for them.

Many things we do not understand simply because we are not yet in a position to do so. This is why patience with other people's experiences and points of view is not only a comfort to them but a relief to us as well. Love overlooks differences, for it notices something of far greater importance: how much like each other we all are because how much like love itself we are. Once we see this honestly, we quickly begin to lose our fear of others and to gain confidence in our potential harmlessness as well. The more we enfold others in this harmlessness, through releasing our own mind of defensiveness and suspicion, the more we begin to glimpse the vast harmlessness of the universe and how utterly impossible it would be for any living thing to suffer for very long in any true sense. There is an end to pain. There is a point beyond which misery cannot go. Never are we left comfortless.

CHAPTER SEVEN

TO GIVE IS TO RECEIVE

The third principle of attitudinal healing presents the fundamental and universal law of possession. There are very few concepts more deeply distrusted than the idea that the only way to keep what is of value is to give it away, and, conversely, that if we try to take from others, we instantly lose. The third principle states:

> **Giving is receiving.** *When our attention is on giving and joining with others, fear is removed and we accept healing for ourselves.*

It is obvious there is still no widespread trust in this idea even though the world frequently gives it lip service. For example, many boys and girls are told a form of this as advice when they begin dating, and adults are sometimes given a more manipulative and indirect version of it in magazines and books that counsel how to win at love and sex.

It was not uncommon in the 1950's for a mother to counsel a

daughter who was going out on a date for the first time that she was responsible for putting her date at ease. As a technique, she was advised to act interested in him and not to try to win his attention by talking about herself. Books and magazine articles of that era suggested that she show this interest by asking questions and finding a subject he would enjoy talking about. She wasn't being advised to listen with her heart but rather to *act* as if she were listening. Nevertheless, even if she began practicing "giving is receiving" in this somewhat dishonest form, she was still likely to discover how easily she could make herself happy while being thoughtful of her date. She found that as she put her date at ease, she also relaxed.

It isn't that we haven't at times experienced the release from anxiety that comes from giving comfort to others but we remain convinced that taking and keeping also have their rewards. We make attempts to be patient and kind and then withdraw our love when our efforts are not properly acknowledged. True giving does not require a sacrifice, but a conflicted approach to giving must be looked at honestly if we are ever to know consistent happiness.

We all have had moments when we were caught up in our own problems, whether physical, emotional or financial, and we were suddenly called upon to help someone in need. Only after the crisis had passed did we notice that our own problems disappeared from our consciousness during the time we were concentrating on helping. They disappeared from our awareness but it is important to note that they may not have disappeared from our life. True healing is not a manipulation of the external situation. It is a change of heart, not a change of circumstances, even though a change of circumstances may accompany it.

When we are concerned with giving, we also receive, because our personal anxieties evaporate from thought. When we recognize that what is in the best interests of another is also of complete benefit to us, we gain inner tranquility, if only briefly, because for that moment we have left our own personal hell behind. The mind simply cannot focus on misery when it is flooded with the desire to heal and make happy, even if the appearances and forms of misery remain.

OUR FOCUS IS
OUR EXPERIENCE

One Tuesday evening when I was meeting with a new adult group at the Center, I discussed some attitudinal healing concepts related to the alleviation of pain. Seated to my left was a woman of about forty named Sarah who said she had metastatic cancer and had not been free of pain for about four months although she was taking large doses of various pain medications.

"Would you be willing to have peace of mind, if only for one second?" I asked. "Yes," she responded, "I haven't had peace of mind for years. How do I get it?" "You have to be willing to look at each person in this room and love them with all the love within you without expecting anything in return," I said.

She said she was willing but she seemed a little doubtful. I asked everyone else in the room if they would also focus their full attention on loving Sarah for just one instant. When everyone agreed, I added that none of us would question Sarah about the results. My reason for saying this was that when we evaluate love, we block our awareness of it because confidence is lacking. Love *is* a state of complete trust based on truth.

When the moment of sharing love was over, the meeting continued as usual. We were saying goodnight a couple of hours later when Sarah suddenly stood up and said, "I can't restrain myself anymore. I have to tell everyone my pain is gone." Then with tears in her eyes, she went around the room and hugged each member of the group.

I believe that what Sarah experienced was a joining through love with something that had before appeared to be outside herself. For a moment she *experienced* the fact that she was not alone. When she was completely involved in extending love, which is her very being, she was not paying attention to her ego and its worries about pain. She actually detached herself from pain by detaching herself from her self-image of weakness, vulnerability, isolation and hopelessness.

What Sarah felt has universal application. The particular form of the physical or psychological distress doesn't matter. In love there is no pain. But it is love we seek and not merely the alleviation of pain.

The term ego, as I use it in this book, stands for the mistaken self-concept that we all hold in thought. It is an image or mental picture of ourselves that is completely inaccurate in what it assumes. We are *not* a thing that is separate and easily hurt. Nor is the reach of our thoughts confined to the boundary of our body. Yet while we focus all our attention on a weak and miserable self-image, as we do most of the time, we block our recognition of what we are. Therefore, we seem to experience all the feelings that a tiny body traveling through a dangerous and uncaring world would experience.

One moment of love, such as the one Sarah experienced, shows us how mistaken our puny self-image can be, for it brings clearly into our mind the fact that we are completely integrated and united with all life and that no form of comfort, help or healing is out of our reach. This cannot be experienced intellectually. Love is required for this shift in experience to be felt. And it *is* practical to seek love rather than a worldly solution to our problems. For love does not preclude action; it makes our actions peaceful.

If you begin by trying to experience this kind of love for as long as five minutes, you may not be able to concentrate and your mind may wander off into its usual activity of comparing and judging. And since the practicing of love is identical to the practicing of peace, it would be destructive to make the control of the mind one more battlefield. It is a pleasant freedom from conflict that is the fertile soil from which love so easily springs. It would be far better for us to content ourselves with comfort than to add tension to our mental processes in the name of love. A good rule for mental conduct is: think whatever makes you truly happy to think.

Once you are successful for one or two seconds, perhaps then you will be encouraged to extend the interval of concentration to several seconds, and, later, to a minute or more. As you continue to retrain your mind, you will eventually find that the experience of love and peace can, on occasion, be extended throughout an entire day.

THE HELP WE GIVE IS OURS

In a very few moments, my father demonstrated to me that even when we give of our health and strength, the results are not that we have less of them, but more. I was having lunch with my parents, who were living in a retirement home, when the following incident occurred.

My father had Parkinson's disease. His symptoms included tremors, difficulty in gait and a masklike facial expression. On this day, he also seemed depressed. Sitting with us at the lunch table was a man his age who was more severely impaired by the same disease than he was. He couldn't walk without help and when his wife didn't come to assist him, he grew impatient and asked my father to help him to his room.

My father took the man's arm and with both of them shaking a great deal, they started to walk. Suddenly, my father began to straighten up and his tremor decreased until it was almost invisible. And he began to smile. About ten minutes later he returned. Once again he was walking in a stooped manner.

"What a remarkable demonstration," I thought. When my father was completely absorbed in helping, he was detached from the symptoms of helplessness. While he was giving strength and stability, he had noticeably more of both. And in addition, he was happy. Once he no longer perceived himself of any use, he returned to a feeble self-concept. And probably all of this happened without his consciously seeing the connection.

Another witness to this cause-and-effect relationship was Paul Johansen. On December 9, 1979, he appeared on "60 Minutes" with Tony Bottarini, another child from the Center. Together they gave the message "teach only love" to over fifty million television viewers. His presence on that program, although unknown to most viewers, was the fulfillment of an agreement he had made with God.

Paul became ill at the age of thirteen and diagnosed himself as having a brain tumor. Subsequent tests proved him right. Later that year, after making out his will, he entered Columbia Presbyterian Hospital in New York City. He was critically ill, had not eaten for a week and was on intravenous fluids. His family and physician did not expect him to live more than a day or two.

Then a miracle occurred. Here is how Paul later described it to me: "It was in the middle of the night and I didn't know whether I was dreaming or having a vision or was awake. I do know I was talking to God. I asked God for a flash so I could have a little more time to help my friends. I told Him I was tired of the pain and suffering. I was tired of fighting my cancer. And I was tired of fighting Him. I said to God that I was willing to let His will be my will, and if I was supposed to die now, that was okay, but I did think I had more to give and I felt He ought to add some extra time. God said He wanted to think about that for a moment. Then He agreed to let me have more time."

The next morning, to everyone's amazement, Paul asked for solid food. In the following days, he began to put on weight and gain strength. Soon, he was able to get into a wheelchair and was discharged from the hospital. Later, he began to walk with a cane and even returned to school.

About this time his mother, Barbara, heard about our program and contacted the Center. Some of the staff and I were scheduled to lecture in New York and we agreed to meet her for lunch in Manhattan. As we talked, she became enthusiastic about our program and expressed a desire for more contact with us. I told her that I would be back in a few weeks to lecture on life and death concepts at Columbia University's College of Physicians and Surgeons and I wondered if Paul might be interested in having me interview him as part of the lecture. We decided that Barbara would ask him and that I would phone her later that week.

Paul agreed. We met one hour before the lecture, but it was as if we had known each other all our lives. Dr. Frank Field, the NBC weatherman and correspondent, happened to be filming a story at the hospital that day. He had heard that our interview was about to take place and asked if he could film it. We said, "Yes," and Paul was a brilliant teacher that day as he told his story about his faith in God and how our purpose here on earth is to serve and help each other. Not only was he helpful to a large medical audience, but that night thousands of people were inspired by his courageous spirit on the television broadcast.

A few months later, Paul and his mother came to Tiburon. He was very excited about going to his first meeting at the Center because he had heard so much about the children. Later, he told his parents that he felt the kids he had met there were more peaceful than any he had known before.

That night Paul and his mother stayed in my home, and the next morning they attended my regular 9:00 A.M. prayer meeting. All of us felt the presence of God in a very special way. When we prayed, as had become our custom, we simply held hands and were silent. Paul commented, "I like your way of praying where there isn't all that talk." Later that day, he said he had been "zapped with energy" from the morning's meeting and that he felt better than he had in weeks.

On another occasion, Paul's sister, Kathleen, and I were talking about him before a large audience at Carleton College in Minnesota. When we were through, I suggested that we and the audience spend a few minutes silently sending love to Paul who was in Connecticut. His parents told me later that at the moment we were praying, Paul felt a rush of energy. He stood up and walked without his cane, something he had not been able to do for months.

This is another example of the healing strength of love and a clear demonstration that minds are not separate. We sometimes forget how strong is this silent form of help. We allow ourselves to slip into a sense of weakness because the one who needs us appears distant and unreachable. It is important to remember that the purpose of silently blessing another is not to try to change some physical ailment but to remind ourselves that love is the connecting link between all the children of God. The passing of love from us to another has an unseen effect on a very deep level. The physical effects Paul experienced are not as important as the love that surrounded him and his family, for this blessing will continue.

The Center kept in frequent telephone contact with Paul and his family. Whenever I was in the East, I would go to Connecticut and visit him. On one of those visits, he was not doing well. He looked pale and depressed. I reminded him that at the Center we believe that sometimes when you are sick, if you will help and love someone, even silently, you can begin to feel happy and your depression will start to disappear. I told him about a new friend of mine, Tony Bottarini, who was ten years old. He had seemed normal in all respects until a few weeks previous when he had developed pain in his leg. It turned out to be bone cancer, and he had to have his leg amputated. I said that I was going to be phoning him at the hospital and perhaps Paul would like to talk with him. I told him I knew he could help.

We placed the call and once again I saw the phenomenon I have seen so many times. As he began to talk with Tony, this young boy, who had looked half dead a few moments earlier, became fully alive. He started telling Tony jokes, and as they talked, a close friendship began to develop between them.

A few weeks later, Al Wasserman, a producer of "60 Minutes," called to say he would like to do a segment on our Center and he asked me for filmable ideas. I told him that a picture of Tony and Paul talking to each other long distance would be a powerful segment and a demonstration of what young people, completely unassisted, could do for each other.

It occurred to me then that this was part of the fulfillment of God's agreement to give Paul a little more time to help others. However, I don't think Paul ever dreamed that the others would mean over fifty million people.

All during his illness, Paul and his family continued to make presentations with me and to help many other people over the phone. On October 17, about 5:00 A.M., I received a phone call from Paul's family telling me he had died peacefully in his sleep.

IT IS ONLY THE GIFT OF
THE HEART THAT MATTERS

The gift we give to others is held within the quiet content of our mind and not just in our words or deeds. Sharon Tennison, a registered nurse, sometimes writes down her experiences and insights and shares them with me, and the following account, which she wrote during a sixteen-hour shift with a patient, illustrates the potential strength and beauty of our silent gifts.

A forty-year-old black male schoolteacher lying quietly in bed . . . a subarachnoid hemorrhage yesterday . . . today he is immobilized, waiting out the bleed in his head. It could abate or blow at any time.

The room is quiet . . . curtains pulled to reduce sensory stimulation . . . vital signs and neuro checks done hourly to monitor his condition . . . ready for any eventuality. The environment is a tense peace, if that is possible.

A little Basque priest comes in making his usual rounds. He inquires quietly about my patient's condition with real concern. I am touched as he walks to the bedrail, holds his hand—palm down—about twelve inches over this man's head, and begins to pray silently. Minutes later he makes a sweeping slow cross over the top part of my patient, and quietly fades out of the room.

I am aware of tears in my eyes. Why does this

touch the heart and soul within me so? This little priest, looking to be in his sixties, salt-and-pepper hair, no taller than 5'3", walks around the hospital comforting the grieving, encouraging the sick and praying with the dying. And here he is today, praying over and loving a sleeping man who doesn't even know him—or know that he is there. And this is his work in the world. He does it with great dignity and compassion.

How many times are there those who are silently holding us in loving thought or prayer when it is completely unknown to us? And I wonder if this might contribute significantly to our life energy. If the scientists and visionaries of the new age are correct, we are linked by a common energy or life force, and the thoughts and energy of one person can affect another.

Which brings me to a haunting possibility—that it does make a difference to every person I am around, or even pass in the hall or on the street, what kind of energy I am emitting. Is it a smile carrying a silent message of love, a quiet acknowledgment that says to them, "I must be worthy. That person thought enough of me to speak?" Or am I throwing out preoccupied energy, keeping in my little mental igloo and encouraging others to do the same? . . . how closed off when I choose the latter . . . how much warmth and understanding when I choose the former.

And my mind slowly comes back from its journey into timeless possibilities, to the bed of this beautiful man, and I take up where the little Basque priest left off, and am so touched and humbled by the possibility that we can enter into each other's lives in this silent way.

Our attempts at giving are dissatisfying if we hold back a part of our love or approval at the time we offer our gift. And this will hold true no matter what form our gift takes because the real gift is the movement of love in our heart. Although our first silent efforts at giving will seem small in light of all there remains to give, even within these efforts we will begin to sense the unlimited treasure within us from which we take. And we will notice another fact: that the more we borrow from our store of love and peace, the more abundantly it grows.

The following letter from Marie Van Lint presents a very clear example of this beautiful and governing principle of all reality. I would like to end this chapter on giving with her letter, so let me make my one comment on it now. It is simply this: Marie Van Lint's *reward* was an inner blessing, not an external one.

. . . I was one of a congregation that overflowed the church. We were there to hear Jerry Jampolsky and others, all very special speakers. The music was beautiful, the feeling vibrant and I was serenely happy to be there.

The contribution basket was passed around and I thought, "How much should I put in?" I had received much; now how much should I contribute? As I usually do when I'm not certain of the answer—and often when I am—I referred the matter to the Holy Spirit. "Holy Friend, how much should I give?"

"Everything," came the quiet answer in my mind.

I was startled. "You're kidding," I said. I had just cashed a fair-sized check and the money was in my wallet. "Look, I was thinking in terms of two to five dollars."

"Everything," said the quiet voice.

I opened my wallet and looked. Twenties, tens, fives—my 'walking around' money for the next two weeks.

"You're sure? All of it?" After all, how could I be sure this was the voice of the Holy Spirit. It could be the voice of ego, of past guilt, of group vibrations; anything.

"Everything."

And I knew I had to go with it. I had always trusted the Voice completely. Not to trust it now meant that I might not trust it for a very long time. There is no such thing as trusting—kind of. You trust or you don't.

So I swallowed hard and reached in my wallet, took out the whole wad and dropped it in the basket. "After all," I thought wryly, "there are still a few coins in the coin purse if I need to feed a parking meter."

"I said everything."

"You really don't let up," I thought as I emptied the few small coins into the basket.

And the most incredible feeling of inner peace and love flooded my heart as the basket passed on. Now I understood that the twenties, the tens, would have been meaningless without the last few coins and that the lesson had nothing at all to do with money.

It was commitment. Total commitment. I could travel light years toward my goal but if I stopped an inch short of it, all the miles would be useless.

That is the gift that was given me. To give all is to receive all. It may seem, on the face of it, that the exchange was totally unequal—spiritual awareness in exchange for some dollars—but I think otherwise. To give the Holy Spirit an instant—The Holy Instant—of absolute trust and commitment is the gift He asks for. It is a great and worthy gift and it is what I had to give. That His gifts to me are so much greater doesn't matter. They are what He has to give.

CHAPTER EIGHT
HEAL THYSELF

 The fourth principle provides the reason why all the other principles of attitudinal healing are true. It reads:

All minds are joined. *Therefore, all healing is self-healing. Our inner peace will of itself pass to others once we accept it for ourselves.*

It is only because minds are joined that healing is inner healing that love cannot be hindered by what is external. That giving to another mind is giving to our own. That freedom is not a function of time. That the strength of every mind is ours. That the voice of love or oneness can always be heard. That all correction is mental. And that love is our only function and destiny.

ALL MINDS ARE JOINED
IN LOVE

Consider for a moment the concept that there is one all-uniting, universal Mind, one all-pervading Intelligence, and consider also its corollary, that there are no totally separate minds. One way this could be imagined is to think of the universe as an ocean. On its surface there are waves. Yet the waves are made by and composed of ocean or water. Now if one wave should suddenly want to separate itself completely from the ocean, to accomplish this it would have to be wholly without water and without any connection with the movement of the ocean. How could it then roll and sparkle or in any way be like a wave? The simple fact is that a wave could not divide itself from the body of all waves and still remain a wave.

Here is another analogy. Once again, water will be our symbol for Mind. Imagine the universe as a vast pool of water, made up entirely of, and completely filled with, water. Now, scoop a bucket of this water up and pour it back in and notice that the movement of part of the water affects every other particle of water in the universe. Notice also that the water that is poured back does not have to be aware of its effect on all the water in the universe in order to have its effect. It has its effect regardless.

Analogies prove nothing, of course, but it is not proof we are seeking. What we want is a broadening of our experience. Each of us is connected to all living things whether we are aware of this beautiful fact or not. It is our unawareness of it that causes all our misery.

We have no private or unaffecting thoughts, *provided the thoughts we have are true or real*. If I, as a mind, am joined with all other minds, I have my influence on others whether or not I wish to. However, if I believe I can separate myself completely from Mind, I am simply self-deceived, for I could no more do this than a wave could separate itself from the ocean and still be a wave. And if a wave could somehow believe that it could accomplish this, that belief would not affect the perfect functioning of the ocean. Any thoughts or emotions I have that are based on the belief that I could cut myself off from Life cannot truly affect Life. In other words, our negative feelings and ideas do not change reality and that is the essential reason why all thoughts of guilt are as groundless as they are unhelpful. But it is also important to see that our fearful and destructive lines of thought do not contribute to our welfare or to the happiness and health of others. What we think is either part of the problem or part of the answer.

There are thoughts that are true and those that are mistaken. The thought of love, for example, is a light that can disperse thoughts of loneliness, illness, pain and depression within our mind. On the other hand, the thoughts of guilt and fear can be very painful for us to entertain but they cannot affect the peaceful core of our being which is love.

Our body is a teaching machine. It will reflect on its screen the feelings and thoughts we program into it. The entry point for all programs is the mind, and what we see reflected throughout the body is what we have put into our mind. Our body will exhibit thoughts that are conflicted and anxious or ones that are peaceful, loving and happy. It has no choice in this, but we do.

This concept can provoke guilt and confusion to the ego. It interprets this simple cause-and-effect relationship as just another opportunity to judge. "If I am sick," it reasons, "I am doing something wrong with my mind." But, of course, this is not entirely accurate. First, the ego is not questioning its own judgments of what is wrong with the body. Second, it is assuming that self-censure is the remedy. And third, it believes that it is up to it alone to correct the focus of the mind. Worrying about how we have been using our mind is merely a way of continuing to misuse it. Fear and regret are never a part of attitudinal healing, because they are a preoccupation with the past and not a loving and relaxing willingness to ask God for help right now.

The body reflects the contents of our mind. If our mind is peaceful, so is our body. But a peaceful state of mind cannot be forced because force is not peaceful. Our mind connects with all other minds, and if our mind is peaceful, peace is the gift we pass along to others. Judging others for being sick or having difficulties is not helpful to them or us. However, if our mind is full of attack thoughts, other minds do not automatically become a helpless victim of our attack. The reason for this is that attack thoughts are based on the belief that other people's minds are separate in purpose and will from ours. When we judge others we are merely attempting to convince ourselves that there could be an advantage to seeing some people as basically unlike us. This idle wish cannot affect reality, and so even though our attack thoughts do nothing to contribute to the comfort of our own bodies or to the ease and joy of others, they do not travel the universe wreaking havoc. They simply partake of, and are a part of, what might be called the collective ego or the collective insanity. They are an utter waste of time and for that reason alone should be of no interest to us.

INNER PEACE PASSES TO OTHERS

Our ego—the fear part of our mind—wants conflict and separateness, which are the food for its survival. Peace and inner quiet are the mortal enemies of the ego. And love and peace are so interwoven with each other that they can never be used separately. We will not have the experience of love encircling us until we have allowed peace within. Yet this peace has nothing whatsoever to do with what is happening in the worldly circumstances around us.

I once heard a beautiful story that can help demonstrate this rule of attitudinal healing. There was a minister in Switzerland, sixty-four years old, near retirement, who began to question his life and his beliefs about God. And as he did so he started having many doubts about himself and his concepts of reality. He became so depressed that he decided to put God on the shelf and get a substitute minister. Attending the local pub became his major activity.

A few days after all these changes had begun, a message came from a woman in his parish saying that her husband had just died. She lived just two doors away and the minister immediately went to her home. He knew exactly what to say because he had been in this situation so many times before. However, just as he began to open his mouth, a little voice inside said, "Say nothing; just think the word peace." About five minutes went by and he started to give his talk again, and again he received the same message. An hour went by and finally the wife began to speak. She said that she could not understand what was happening. Her husband was dead in bed and she was experiencing more peace than she ever had in her life. He told her that he also was experiencing peace as never before. He felt for the first time that he knew what the peace of God was.

Let us remember each day, each minute, each second, and let us remember especially in the morning as we rise, that when we accept peace for ourselves, peace is received to some degree by all others in this world. This is the way the world will become transformed, and not by our attacking those who are in favor of attack.

BODILY CONDITIONS CANNOT BLOCK TRUE COMMUNICATION

We protect our mental privacy, or sense of separateness, in many ways. One that I run across frequently in my work is the belief that deep and meaningful communication with another is *already* blocked because of some bodily state or condition. The age of the body, physical damage to the brain, differences in ethnic or social backgrounds, autism, language barriers and inebriation are just a few examples of differences between bodies that appear to keep minds divided. But none of these physical states are the barriers they seem because actual communication and all the benefits that flow from it pass between our love center and the love center of other people completely unaffected by the education, training, age or condition of our brains. I recognize that this statement is not an obvious truth to most; however, the consistent, straightforward practicing of love in an individual's life will bring all the evidence of its truth that he could possibly want, and after a time, all arguments that minds are not in communication will be seen as merely silly.

I would like you to read another account by nurse Sharon Tennison that beautifully illustrates the fact that we are joined, on a very deep level, and that bodily states of any type cannot impede actual communication.

It's a mid-December day . . . Christmas presents already made or bought . . . my children busy for the evening . . . and I have nothing planned. I call one of the hospitals to see if they need help for the evening shift. As usual they do.

Floating from hospital to hospital and working on any floor or intensive care unit can be an exciting adventure. One never knows what kind of medical, emotional or spiritual crisis the next eight hours will bring or what sort of personalities one will get to know by the end of the shift. On the way to the hospitals my heart usually finds itself putting out a little prayer that I will be placed where my personality can be most useful or where I can learn something that my brain or soul needs. Then the matter is dropped and I assume, wherever the placement is, that is where I am supposed to be.

This particular night the assignment is on a medical floor. During report from the off-going nurse, I learn about a very irascible patient in room 322. He is a forty-four-year-old man (my age) in end-stage alcoholic disease who gets back at the world by all sorts of antisocial acts; the most recent is refusal to ask for the bedpan, making it necessary for the staff to be constantly changing linens. He is hostile and combative and requires body and wrist restraints. The day nurse is ready to be rid of him, and I am not at all sure about taking him on, along with eight other pretty sick patients.

Rounds of my rooms are made, and on approaching room 322 a strong odor of formaldehyde floats through the air. It becomes offensive as I enter the room. The curtains are pulled tight around 322-B. I peek in and there in the bed is a shriveled-up little body rolled up in fetal position with blankets piled high, smelling for the world like one of my anatomy or physiology lab experiments. I pull some cover away from his face to get his attention, and he doesn't appear to rouse. On my third attempt to rouse him, he hurls verbal abuse, grabs his blanket and disappears under it again.

I stand there looking at this little heap of humanity, reflect on my own healthy body, and wonder how this can happen to someone in forty-four years. That he is my own age seems to put a stronger bond between us in my heart. How could it have happened?

I walk out and continue from room to room until I have some idea about the rest of my patients for the night. They are fairly stable, emotionally in good places and have family members around for support and love. Only my little man in 322 . . . I check with the desk . . . no, he never has visitors. On checking his drug cards I see he is receiving Paraldehyde, 10cc. intra-muscularly every six hours for delerium tremens and this is the reason for his offensive odor.

Dinner trays are brought at 5:00 P.M. I go to his room to see if he is able to feed himself. He doesn't even know the tray is there. Slowly I get adjusted to the now darkening room with the curtains still pulled tightly around the bed. I put a spoon of jello to his mouth gently and to my surprise he takes it in. Then another. And another. My mind is still puzzling and wondering if there is any way to reach this little withdrawn soul. My heart tells me probably the only thing he would register to is just loving gentle service. When he has had enough jello he pulls the cover up over his mouth and again disappears without a word. I remove his tray from the room and continue on with the duties of the night.

At 6:00 P.M. it is time for his Paraldehyde. Five cc's in each buttock—a huge dose for the muscle to take—and I dread doing this to this already pained little man. I proceed to his room with the two syringes drawn full. As I enter, I realize the formaldehyde smell is mixed with another. He has fought back at the world again—perhaps in the only method left to him, since his hands are restrained and his days numbered. Part of working with humanity at this level is that your senses become dulled when necessary.

The room is now almost dark . . . a very faint night light is overhead . . . and I find myself standing there silently beside the curtained bed. Little remembrances start coming through my mind: words of Dr. Jerry Jampolsky whom I heard recently talking about 'the most offensive people are in the greatest need of love,' and thoughts of 'extending love,' of 'letting loose of the evaluator in myself,' of 'looking at this little man, really looking at him, and making him my brother.' And knowing of nothing else to do, I just let these thoughts be active in the space between us, almost a trance like quiet. And something wells up in my heart, a different feeling, a realization, and somewhere deep inside me a knowing comes that perhaps this little man has never been touched in his entire forty-four years. Perhaps he was a poor little Mexican boy, the last one of a large family, born in some dusty, confused, frustrated place where migrant workers fight for survival. I could see a skinny little boy coming up in this world with no skills, no support, no love—and perhaps the bottle was the only consolation he had found in life. Was this little boy in the vision in my mind or could it have been one of those rare intuitions? I don't know or really care because it does make me see into the possibility of my patient and feel a deep empathy that seems to well up from my very bones.

I reach down to lift the black hair out of his eyes. He doesn't move. Again I put my hand to his forehead and clear more hair away. The least I could give to this little boy in my head is the touch that perhaps he never received before. Then, as I sit down on his bed, my heart simply takes over and my hands comfort in a simple kind of way. The mixed smells of the room have disappeared from my awareness and the syringes go patiently waiting.

There is a sense of being caught up in some place somewhere between the everyday and the heavenly planes, a place of the Now where nothing else matters except the moment. At some point, I hear myself saying to him, in a voice more loving than my normal voice, "I know if you had another chance to live your life over, you wouldn't choose the bottle." It sounds like a strange thing to say once it is out, but must have been the right thing. A hushed and sorrowful voice comes back, "Oh, no, ma'm"—so permeated with feeling and sadness. He then begins haltingly to tell me that he has been drinking since a teenager in El Paso, Texas. His has been a hard border town life from the beginning. "I hate the taste. I drink to forget my misery." Somewhere in the conversation I ask if he thinks there is anything we can do to help him work with his addiction, and he tells me no, that it is like a monster. He knows he will go back to it if he lives this time to leave the hospital.

I consider this: that everything in my nursing skills is directed to helping people see their life problems, helping them gather the resources to begin to combat their limitations, offering the support and love and encouragement that makes them believe in themselves again—and yet this is not useful here. My heart just loves this little man. Whether he can quit alcohol or not is not material to me. He is precious, and by some quirk of fate, I have been allowed to see into him and love him somewhere deep where alcohol doesn't touch. And I share with him that I know what a battle life has been for him and that I understand if he can't quit— and it is okay—that I find him a very special person and want to do anything for him I can to make him comfortable. By this time we are holding hands and an incredible amount of feeling permeates the room.

I begin to become aware of another reality: the bed needs to be changed and the injections are over thirty minutes late. But what has happened is more important. I am sensing that this little soul may have to leave this crippled body, but may go into eternity knowing that he has experienced love and acceptance.

And as for me, I walk out of the room on my way to get fresh linens, and hear myself exclaiming, "Oh, Jesus, this is how you must feel—about all the children of Earth—as we get caught in the webs of limitations, and get lost. You see beyond all this into the core of our very being." *So this is how unconditional love feels.* It is my first experience at this depth, and I feel lifted into another dimension by being allowed to share in this oneness.

We untie this little man, no longer combative, and change his bed. He apologizes for the extra work. There is a new feeling in the room, and I have a fresh realization of how mountains of depression and frustration can be leveled through the extension of love.

CHAPTER NINE
WHY NOT NOW?

The present is the only time we can decide between love and fear. When we worry about what we should do in the future, we accomplish nothing. And yet, our mental habit of rewriting the past and rehearsing what is to come does generate various forms of pain. A mental shift back into the present helps remove the source of misery. The fifth principle of attitudinal healing states this concept in the following way:

Now is the only time there is. *Pain, grief, depression, guilt and other forms of fear disappear when the mind is focused in loving peace on this instant.*

There is usually a tremendous preoccupation with the past and future when we are suffering from illness or pain. We are tempted to look at all our past misery and wonder how long we are now going to have to endure *this*. When we are ill and hurting, it often doesn't feel like anyone is loving us. To the contrary, it feels like we are being punished or in some other way attacked for something we suspect is our own fault. Consequently, we may spend most of our time focused on our body, measuring the sickness and pain, wondering what we did to deserve this, and predicting that the next movement will surely be like the last. And, of course, we tend to make ourselves right about these predictions.

As I have stated many times in this book, I have been impressed with how quickly pain can disappear when we direct our mind outside ourselves in a caring way to others. Let me tell you about Randy Romero. He was a twenty-five-year-old who was hospitalized with cancer. His pain was difficult to control even though he was on high doses of morphine (over 100mg. hourly). He had been very active in sports and had helped children at our Center in a project that allowed them to meet famous sports figures.

Shortly before he died, I asked Randy, "Of all the people you have heard about in sports, what person would you like to meet most of all, if it were possible?" He replied, "Bernard King." Randy admired him not only because of his excellence as a performer but because he had whipped a drug problem and now was helping others.

I didn't know anyone in the Golden State Warriors office but I phoned anyway. The results came quickly. By 2:30 the next day, Bernard King was visiting Randy. From someone bedridden and immobilized with pain, Randy turned into a young man filled with enthusiasm. He had his picture taken with Bernard; they talked about drugs and laughed together as they walked down the hall in each other's arms. Randy had no pain during that two and a half hours, and later his mother told me that he said it had been one of the happiest days of his life. He died peacefully two weeks later.

There is so much we can do for others, and for that very reason, there is so much we can do for ourselves. Randy and Bernard received love simply because they gave so much of it. In the process, fear and pain disappeared. If it is true that only now is real, then the past cannot hurt us, and will not unless we make it a part of our present. The mind can always be put to love rather than to one more review of what is already finished. Let bygones be bygones; let love be now.

GUILT IS A DENIAL OF THE PRESENT

Our present mental decisions are the sole determiner of our present experience. Because this statement is so foreign to how we usually approach life, I would like to give you another illustration of it, this time from my own experience.

One day while brushing my teeth, I sneezed. My back went into acute spasm and I fell to the floor, screaming in agony. I was hospitalized, had many examinations and was told I had organic back syndrome. I was put in traction and given drugs. Two weeks later, I left the hospital feeling better but still in pain. For the next five years I don't think I was ever free of it. My physician advised me to stop all physical exercise—tennis, basketball, jogging, skiing, gardening—which were all activities I loved.

As the years went by, the chronic nature of my condition became increasingly apparent. I was going to have to learn to adapt myself to the disability. Surgery might be helpful but there was no guarantee.

Later, I began to notice that my back seemed to be a barometer of even the slightest emotional stress. But I tricked myself into believing that my reaction to stress was not a fundamental cause of the pain because I possessed x-rays which showed that my condition was organically caused. At one point my back became so bad that I was hospitalized again. The consulting neurosurgeon strongly recommended surgery. He went so far as to say that without it my pain would never disappear. As I was facing that decision, I suddenly saw the truth, which had been there all the time.

I realized that behind my back pain was a complex of thoughts that included anger, resentment, fear and guilt, all of which were my personal ties to the past. These feelings appeared to be caused by longstanding conflicts in my marital relationship. I saw that I was angry at my wife for not supplying what I felt I lacked and for not meeting my needs. And yet I was feeling guilty about having such angry thoughts about her and believed I deserved to be punished for them. The back pain also gave me an excuse to drink more when the drugs were not effective. I decided that rather than undergo surgery I would try to undo the cause of the pain in another way.

I am not saying that surgery is either right or wrong. My decision to forego it was simply the one I personally needed at the moment to refocus my mind. The body, by itself, is not what is important. Therefore, we do whatever allows us to let go of our preoccupation with it and return to peace. It is our goal of peace this instant that will indicate how to care for our body this instant. We simply do what the aim of sustaining and deepening our inner happiness dictates. Such an approach is far superior to making unbending decisions for the future because we are then tempted to consult our former decisions rather than our sense of peaceful preferance that is always available to us.

As a result of my new insights and my determination to pursue them, my back problems improved but did not go away. After my divorce, I found that the stress of other situations or relationships were also displaced onto my body. One weekend, years later, I was almost hospitalized because of an acute attack. It was a classic example of how guilt finds the most symbolic part of our body in which to manifest itself.

I was attending a conference in Virginia where I met a very attractive and intelligent woman. We immediately became intimately involved. It seemed like two lost souls coming home. But my newfound friend turned out to be married, and I very quickly began to experience tremendous feelings of guilt.

After the conference she invited me to New York to have dinner with her and her husband the next time I came to New York. In my state of rising guilt, meeting her husband was the last thing I wanted to do. Yet another part of me yearned to be with her one more time, so I changed my original flight plans and flew to New York.

As I picked up my suitcase at Kennedy Airport, an acute pain shot through my back and I collapsed. I managed to get to the airport bar where I had more than a few drinks. Later, I got a taxi and went to my hotel. Severe back spasms continued and I returned to San Francisco the next day in agony. It was a full month before I was free of pain.

After I was introduced to A Course in Miracles, I began to realize how attached to guilt I was. I became aware that this attachment caused me to fear love, which is the same thing as fearing the present. As I learned to let go of guilt and anxiety, I found a new sense of well-being. I decided that as best I could I would no longer allow myself to be limited by my judgments of the past and my fears of the future. But I saw that I couldn't do this alone; I *had* to ask God's help in making such a radical break with what had become my habitual way of thinking.

I am now actively involved in physical activities that I once had been told I would never be able to participate in. However, I want you to know that I am not consistent in practicing these spiritual principles. There are many times I am tempted to judge and make decisions about the future. When I do, and my mind is not in harmony, I will sometimes feel tension in my back. Then, I look for the unforgiving thought beneath the pain. I quiet my mind and tell myself I want the peace of God more than anything else. I pray, asking my inner Teacher for help in forgiving, and I give thanks that I am joined to everyone in love. When I do this, I often find that the back tension disappears, but more importantly, I again feel God's loving and constant presence.

NOW IS ANOTHER NAME FOR LOVE

It might be helpful to examine the mental process behind my episodes of back pain a little more closely. Back pain itself is very common in our society, and yet all physical pain is produced in a very similar way, and, likewise, its remedy is basically the same.

The fifth principle links freedom from pain with awareness of the present. Certainly, everyone thinks he is aware of the present, and it is true that most of us do see the objects and hear the sounds that surround us. But notice that the fifth principle states that pain and other forms of fear disappear only when the mind is *focused* in love on this instant. If we are *using* the people around us only as a means of recalling the past, we can hardly claim to be focusing our loving attention on them.

It was a small step in the right direction for me to associate my back pain with my judgmental attitudes toward my wife, rather than with just a deteriorated disk, but it was a mistake for me to believe that the years of conflict within our marriage were somehow responsible for my *present* anger. Guilt produces projection, and projection is simply a way of shifting blame rather than letting go of blame. And because projection is a form of attack, it makes us feel even more guilty and so we continue punishing ourselves in some form.

If we are merely seeing people as they are now, we are currently practicing forgiveness. But if looking at them is only our excuse for recalling their past mistakes, then they have become a means for hurting us. Our new practice should be the consistent cleansing of our vision of all past associations. We constantly free all we see of negative and limiting memories.

The cycle of feeling guilty, shifting blame to others, getting angry at the guilt we now see in them, attacking them for their guilt, feeling even more guilty for our attack and punishing our bodies in payment, cannot be escaped as long as we believe in guilt as a valid description of anything. We must make a decision for innocence if we are ever to have consistent mental peace and the resulting bodily peace. The innocence of another cannot be found in his past behavior. It may even be hard to see within what his body is presently doing. But it can be found in the peace that is within *us*. It is viewed past the personality, past bodily behavior, and past our mental associations. It is like a light that shines within our heart and the heart of the other person, and once it is glimpsed it will be far more real to us than our or the other person's guilt, because it *is* more real. To undertake the search for innocence is basically all we need to do to gradually free ourselves of pain, grief, depression, guilt and other forms of fear.

Several months ago, I was asked to see a woman in her late fifties who had cancer of the brain. When I arrived at her home, I first spent some time with Ed, her husband. He told me his family had been fortunate because no one had ever been seriously ill prior to this. So it was quite a shock when his wife was diagnosed as having cancer. She had been operated on but the cancer was not removable. Despite chemotherapy and x-ray treatment, the prognosis was guarded.

Ed said he had come from a poor family with many children. When he was seven years old there wasn't enough food to feed everyone, and he pledged to himself that this would never happen to his family when he grew up. As a young man, he went into business for himself, worked long hours and was rarely home. His wife had raised their two children largely by herself. Ed became quite wealthy; his son joined him in the business, and life seemed satisfactory until his wife became ill. When that happened, he decided, for the first time in their marriage, to spend more time at home.

One day their gardener said to him, "One of the rosebushes in the garden looks like it has died. Is it all right if I pull it out and replace it?" Ed thought a moment, then said he would like to see it. As he stood looking down at the bush, it occurred to him that he had one of the loveliest rose gardens in the city, yet in the last twenty years he had never taken time to enjoy it.

"Don't pull it out. It *is* alive and I would like to care for it myself," he said. Daily, Ed visited the garden to love, nourish and water the rosebush. It began to come back to life, and several weeks later a beautiful rose appeared. Ed snipped it off and took it to his wife, whose name, of course, was Rose.

Because of how he chose to respond to his wife's illness, Ed was now able to realize how much of life he had let pass him by.

He had been so preoccupied with accumulating more money for the future that he had forgotten to live in the present.

After hearing that surprising story, I talked to Rose. I asked what was going on in her life before she developed cancer; had there been any stress preceding the onset? She said no, she and her husband and children had been perfectly happy. A few minutes later, however, tears came to her eyes and she shared some very significant information. When Ed first went into business twenty-five years ago, her brother became his partner. The following year Ed bought her brother's share of the business, but the brother felt he had not received enough money in the financial arrangement and hadn't spoken to either Ed or her since.

Rose stated that she loved both her brother and her husband, but felt loyalty to her husband. Through the intervening years, she had a nagging sense of guilt that she should resolve the conflict. She was depressed about the situation but had never talked about it until now. I explained to her how important I thought it was for her to resolve this. Otherwise, she might have some ambivalence about ever being happy again because she would know she would still have to face a life situation that she found painful. We talked about forgiveness, not only between her brother and husband but also for herself. She gave me permission to bring Ed in and speak with both of them about it.

It was difficult for Ed to believe that the wife he knew so well had kept this from him while feeling such conflict for all these years. He immediately went to the phone to call her brother to ask forgiveness. The next day there was a reconciliation.

So Rose, like Ed, was not living in the present, even though the way they had avoided the present had taken different forms. Their joint recognition of the beauty and harmony, always inherent in the living moment, allowed their relationship to bloom, and for the remaining months that Rose lived, they were immeasurably happier.

NOTHING IS NEEDED
TO BE HERE NOW

To live peacefully and happily in the present is so very simple that when we first become aware of it, we stand in disbelief at all we put ourselves through before. How easy to forget the past and future and be content now. What do we do that makes it all so difficult? Here are three common ways we add unnecessary complexities and complications to our lives, along with suggestions on how to return to simplicity and peace:

1. If we fear the world, we will be hesitant to do anything without considering all the consequences. And since it is impossible to move even a chair without ramifications, anxiety accompanies even the smallest events of each day. How simple it is to acknowledge that we are not in a position to see the outcome of anything and that all the worry in the world could not control the future. How simple it is to see that we can only be happy now and that there will never be a time when it is not now. We *will* endlessly complicate our lives when our focus is on results. It is only the effort that we control. Success lies in *how* we try and not in our or other people's appraisal of the effect. If we would take just half the time we spend worrying about ramifications and use it instead on direct action, nothing important would go undone. Simplicity lies in putting effort before results.

2. As a baby struggles to learn to walk, he never pauses to analyze why he just fell down. With each fall, an adjustment is automatically made. The baby instinctively knows that he is *being* taught and never tries to teach himself lessons he does not understand. Adults, on the other hand, spend a remarkable portion of their lives going over and

over each mistake in a vain attempt to codify what has in fact already been internally assimilated. How simple it is to resign as our own teacher. How easy it can be to turn quickly from the past because the present is where our life is taking place.

3. Learning to respond to now is all there is to learn, and we are not responding to this instant if we are judging any aspect of it. The ego looks around for what to criticize. This always involves a comparison with the past. But love looks upon the world peacefully and accepts. The ego searches for shortcomings and weaknesses. Love watches for any sign of light and strength. It sees how far each one has come and not how far he has to go. How simple it is to love and how exhausting it is to always find fault, for every time we see a fault we think something needs to be done about it. Love knows that nothing is ever needed but more love.

CHAPTER TEN

THE PEACEFUL PREFERENCE

As we begin practicing a more loving approach to life it will still seem that all our difficulties have great meaning and that we must take clear cut positions for or against every issue surrounding each of them. These stands obviously get in the way of our desire to be nonjudgmental, and yet how can we avoid taking them? Clearly we can't unless we were to withdraw from life altogether.

That someone would actively seek after a thing that has no connection with the problems of life seems incomprehensible to our ego. When I explain to people that the Center gives no treatment, one of the most common responses is, "Oh, I see, you help children adjust to pain and death." And this is indeed a reasonable assumption, but it is not attitudinal healing.

Attitudinal healing recognizes a reality that is not connected to troubles, upsets, or even tragedies. That reality is love. And love is entered and assimilated only as our mind loses interest in either fighting against or succumbing to the miseries of life. When the significance of this fact about love first begins to dawn on us, our initial reaction is likely to be one of confusion about how we are to behave, because our tendency is always to want to know in what way truth is supposed to be applied to life. And, of course, the truth of love cannot be applied; it can only fill our heart. Once this is done we will instinctively act in an appropriate way.

A center for children with catastrophic illness that does not have the goal of either healing the body or adjusting the mind to accept the illness is clearly not asking those who come to it to behave in any particular way. Attitudinal healing is not concerned with behavior, and this has occasionally been frustrating to some who have wished that we take a stand either for or against a particular treatment, system, diet or regime. Our "stand" is that the individual has within him the resources to make that decision for himself, and we are there to help him and ourselves enter more deeply into that place of strength and understanding.

How then should a person who wishes to live in a more loving way go about making decisions? The sixth principle of attitudinal healing addresses itself to this question.

Decisions are made by learning to listen to the preference of peace within us. *There is no right or wrong behavior. The only meaningful choice is between fear and love.*

THERE MUST BE A BETTER WAY

In this book, I have frequently pointed out how our decisions are usually made: by judging the situation and consulting the past for what we are to change and how we are to change it. It is always the situation, or the people within it, that appears to need correcting. If we are counseled to shift our concern from the outward picture to our own mental state, this may require a degree of trust that we are not in the habit of exercising. But surely it is obvious that if we continue running our lives strictly along the lines that our personal past dictates, nothing new can enter them. By declining to judge—that is, to apply standards based solely on the past—we can look directly at what is happening and turn to this other reality within us, which is not attached to our old experiences, and receive a fresh insight. Our own very short history does not hold vast caches of wisdom. In fact, it is so personal in its bias and so distorted in how we now picture it that it is really of little use to us.

I know of no story that better illustrates this point than that of Aeeshah Ababio. Here is an inspiring example of our capacity to turn from personal history toward the voice of happiness that can be heard within our heart.

Aeeshah has worked closely with all of us at the Center for several years. Her gifts of love and humor and her special insights have transformed many lives, young and old. And yet it was not very long ago that working this intimately with whites would have been unthinkable for her. The following is her account of how this major shift in her perception occurred.

Before I became a student of A Course in Miracles, I was a Black Muslim and believed that only some of the people on earth were children of God. I felt it was necessary to separate myself from those who were un-Godlike, and I had no idea that with this attitude I was limiting myself from experiencing the totality of God's presence. I believed that if God had wanted everyone to be brothers and experience brotherly love, He would have included all people in the African Ethnicity.

I had an enormous amount of love in my heart; however, it was only shared with a portion of the people on earth, and I added further to my confusion by teaching this lesson to others. I taught love *and* fear. I told my people that Whites were to be feared and hated because they were not children of God due to the color of their skin. As a result, *my* experiences with the people of this earth were mixed with love and fear, and I did not experience the totality of God's love.

You may wonder how I came out of this confused state of mind. I did not do it alone. I was helped by my internal teacher, whom I now refer to as the Holy Spirit.

While on this path of spiritual confusion, I would experience moments in which I would sense an inner urge to know more and to be more than what had been shown me thus far. Books would come to me that were unrelated to my chosen path, but they spoke of another path which dealt with the concept of the Oneness of God. These books stirred within me a longing that I was not fully capable of fulfilling. My desire to be at one with God was like a tiny light in a dark room, and I began to question my belief system. I wondered: 'How could there be a Oneness of God if some are excluded?' The more I opened myself to experiencing this Oneness, the more I perceived within my chosen path a weakness that could not withstand the test of reason.

One day, in a moment of inner turmoil, I asked, 'If there is a Oneness in God, how can I experience it?' No sooner had I asked than an answer began to come to me. It was a Sunday afternoon and I was reading the *Tribune*. On the front page was an article announcing a psychic seminar to be held at a nearby university. As I read, a voice from within me clearly told me that I was to attend this seminar. I was puzzled because I had never felt an inner voice. While I concentrated on what had transpired, again I heard, 'Go.'

The following morning I telephoned the institution where the seminar was to be held. I spoke with the secretary who immediately referred me to the director of their program. I introduced myself and requested an appointment with him. He said he would be pleased to meet with me, and we made an appointment for the following afternoon.

I arrived a bit apprehensive about my reason for being there, and I went into the administrative office simply to get the appointment over with. The secretary informed me that the director was expecting me and took me into his office. I sat there wondering what this man thought of me. Did he think I was crazy because my dress code wasn't acceptable in the wider society? Did he wonder why this Black Muslim would come to see him? All kinds of thoughts ran across my mind. As I sat in a chair directly in front of him, he was very patient as I fumbled through my purse to get the news clipping about the psychic seminar. He asked very quietly, "How may I help you?" I began talking non-stop about my chosen spiritual path, and that I was guided to attend this conference, and asked if it was possible for me to come. I added that I did not have any money and I knew that there was a fee to attend.

He had listened very attentively, nodding his head as if he understood. Then he said, "You can attend, but you will have to agree to pay the fee at a later date." I agreed and left his office feeling a sense of accomplishment.

The following Sunday I found myself seated in a large auditorium filled with the people whom I had been taught to fear and hate because they were un-Godlike. I moved forward to the front row so that the population I was in the midst of would not preoccupy my mind. I sat down and pulled my hat over my forehead so that my eyes would be shaded, and folded my arms as a sign that I was to be on guard.

The day began with parapsychologists presenting information intended to bind the gap between psychology and spirituality. Their presentations were informative but dull. Finally, a lady named Judith Skutch came up who was introducing a set of books entitled A *Course in Miracles*. As she began to read the introduction, I again heard an inner voice which said, 'This is a tool for you, dear child, use it and I will guide your way. For I am with you always.' This lady began to glow, and again I was told, 'This is your sister, whom I love dearly.' I was filled with love in my heart for this lady. I also felt at home and safe. This was a very strange experience for me because this lady was from among those people whom I believed were un-Godlike. Yet a voice deep within me spoke of God's love for her. I sat quietly after her presentation, thinking about what had transpired. I no longer could base my separatist belief on anything I felt, because all I felt at that moment was unconditional love for all of the children on the earth. At that moment, God's love entered my heart and dispelled any false belief I had held about any of His children.

It wasn't easy to sustain that transcended perception about my surroundings, and I began to feel doubt about my feeling of Oneness. I felt good inside but I still wasn't sure if I should be experiencing love without measuring and evaluating. 'Were these books necessary?' was a question that persisted in my consciousness. Why should I trust that one experience as a valid reason to purchase a set of books that I had never examined closely?

I sat in my seat for a prolonged period observing people moving toward the back of the auditorium, purchasing books from a man who was smiling and being very polite. I consciously felt that it would be a wild goose chase to buy these books with the idea that they would serve some useful purpose in my spiritual process. I looked at all the people in the auditorium and judged against them. Then I slowly walked to the back of the room and inquired about the cost. The man informed me in an unusually warm manner that they had sold all the books on hand. I felt relieved and thought this was a sign that I wasn't supposed to have them. Just as I was about to turn away, he said to me that his name was Jerry Jampolsky and if I wanted them I could come to a meeting at his home on Thursday evening. He gave me the directions I would need. I left the seminar feeling very confused about my chosen spiritual path. I also felt a sense of being comforted by a still, small voice saying, 'Be still, my child, and know that I am with you always.'

At that time, my circle of friends and supporters consisted of others who were in the same thought system as myself. I wondered with whom I could possibly share this experience. How could I tell them that I wanted to go to the home of someone we felt must be avoided so that we would not be deceived? I knew I did not want to go alone, but I did want to go. As I pondered my situation, again, for only a moment, I heard a still voice saying, 'Don't worry about who shall go, for that is already taken care of.' I relaxed and made a choice not to rebuke this voice.

The next day a dear friend called to inquire about the psychic seminar. I shared with her my interest in *A Course in Miracles*, and that I wanted to purchase these books, but I would have to go to Tiburon on Thursday evening. She was interested but unsure about going. I shared with her that I did not really want anyone else to know because we would have to be among people who were not children of God. When she heard that, she decided that she could not possibly let me go alone.

I spent the rest of the week wrestling with my split mind. Was I crazy? Here I was wanting to go into the midst of beings whom I thought diabolical. Why was I going there? To get a set of books that a voice inside me insisted would guide me home. All of this did not really make any sense. But I knew that I would go.

On Thursday we arrived at Jerry Jampolsky's home and he greeted us with a warm smile. Of course, I was suspicious of his warm regard for me. His home was filled with people, all of whom were classified by me as Satan's children. I saw myself as separate from everyone in the room except my friend; however, the room was very crowded and we were forced to separate. I found myself sitting quietly between two strange bodies that were unlike mine.

Once seated, our first instruction was to hold hands and sense our inherent connectedness. As I stretched forth my hands to the two people next to me, I closed my eyes to blot out the presence of their white bodies. My mind was active with fear thoughts, fears of the past, fears of oppression and racial strife. And fear that the children of God *were* connected and not separate.

I felt the grasp of their hands over mine. Then, as I began to breathe deeply, relaxing in the environment I was in, for a moment I began to feel loved and safe. And I was, to my surprise, sending love out to the people who were next to me, and I could sense this loving energy moving out to everyone in that room. Again, I heard deep within me, 'My child, teach only love for this is what you are.' I felt safe and at home. At that moment, I knew that everyone in that room was my brother and I was one with them. As I opened my eyes, these bodies whom I had perceived as enemies were transformed into friends and loved ones.

BEHAVIOR FOLLOWS PEACE

Consistent peace is not the same as regimented behavior. Our behavior should follow our peace of mind like a wake trailing the movements of a ship. If peace is our single aim in all we do, we will always know what to do because we will do whatever will protect and deepen our peace. This approach is in marked contrast to the exhausting attempt to decide every movement beforehand on the basis of whether it will turn out right.

Our ego always wants to see its way clear before it acts. It prefers mental conflict now to simple action. It would rather pause and stew than move easily forward, and so it uses its favorite delaying tactic: the question of right and wrong.

Everyone wants to be moral and good, at least in his own terms, and so the ego uses this desire to engage our attention in an interminable calculation of consequences. Yet it is only now that we can be good, kind and gentle. No way exists in the present to accurately determine the future effect of the least of our actions. And it goes without saying that there is no way for us to go back in time and correct what we consider to be our past mistakes. No matter how long we try, we will not know all the people our actions will affect or whether the effect will be beneficial in the long run. Why then engage in an impossible task, no matter how well meaning it may seem, when genuine opportunities to be kind and truly helpful are all around us?

Understanding this releases us from a guilty preoccupation with the future and gives us permission to consult the present urgings of peace and love within our heart. Yet it must be stressed that as we start out, this procedure will require trust. We simply begin to do what our sense of peace indicates, even though we do not know the outcome. Of course, we never knew the outcome before, but we did have a certain sense of safety in thinking we had second-guessed the results. Now we admit that a loving preference is a more reliable basis for a decision than guesses about future consequences.

Several months ago I met with Carol Chapman and her daughter, Hillary, who was hospitalized with a brain tumor at Children's Hospital in Los Angeles. Two weeks later, I received a phone call from Carol. She said Hillary was now going in and out of a coma and that when her daughter was lucid she would beg her to take her off chemotherapy and x-ray treatment. Carol was very distressed and asked me what she should do. I told her that if she had asked me this kind of question a few years ago I would have known exactly what to advise her. Now, I said, the only thing I knew to say to her was what I would tell myself: to be still and listen to her inner voice. For I had learned from experience that the one thing that could bring a restful assurance in an extreme and painful dilemma such as this was the Voice of Peace itself.

My response did not satisfy her. She said she knew I was an expert in these matters and should therefore be able to give her a definite course of action. We talked awhile longer, but she was still unhappy with me when we hung up.

The next day Carol called me again, and this time her voice was quite serene. She told me that after we talked, she was able to quiet her mind and pray. And this, she said, was the answer she received: "There is no right or wrong. There is only love." The answer freed her mind from fear and allowed her to consult deeply her love for her daughter. What she then saw that she wanted to do was stop all treatments as her daughter had requested.

Three weeks later, Hillary died a very peaceful death. Carol received the news at a conference where several other parents who had lost children to cancer were present, and they were able to comfort her in a way that only parents who have been through it could.

Once we realize there is no right or wrong procedure, we can turn to love in complete confidence. But the peaceful preference that lies within our heart cannot be heard until we have relinquished our fearful emphasis on specific answers. First, we must see that any number of alternatives could be accompanied by the peace and love we desire. We see that we do not care personally which course of action we take, but that we do care that our way be kind, harmless and harmonious. Now our emphasis is on how we go, not where we go. And from this type of inner calm will always come a simple suggestion as to what to do. Our part is to gently do it so that we can enter once more into peace. And if a change or another course of action is needed later, we are not afraid to take it.

Instead of judging everything and trying to twist people and circumstances into appearances we like, the way of peace proceeds quietly and simply. Whenever life surprises us, our first reaction is now to consult that calm place within our heart. We stop and rest a moment in God's love. Then, if action is needed to restore our peace of mind, we take the course that comes to us from out of our calmness. We act with assurance, for indeed we have been assured. And if later we need to ask again, we do so quickly and easily. Our purpose is not to seek peace in order to make rigid decisions or set for ourselves long term rules, but rather to make those decisions that will return us to peace this instant. For it is only when we are peaceful that we can be truly kind.

CHAPTER ELEVEN

FORGIVENESS HAS NO STOPPING POINT

Forgiveness is the means whereby we experience peace, know ourselves as love, give without sacrifice, join with the essence of others, experience fully this instant, and hear clearly the inner counselings of happiness. Forgiveness is the way all the rules of attitudinal healing are understood and applied. The last principle is:

> **Forgiveness is the way to true health and happiness.** *By not judging, we release the past and let go of our fears of the future. In so doing, we come to see that everyone is our teacher and that every circumstance is an opportunity for growth in happiness, peace and love.*

In this book I do not use the word forgiveness the way it is commonly used. Here, it does not mean to repress our anger and act as if everything is acceptable when all the while we are feeling that it isn't. Nor, of course, does it mean to act out our anger. And above all, it does not mean that we assume a position of superiority and pardon sins that we believe are real. Or as my friend, Bill Thetford, puts it: "Bring the guilty bastard in so I can forgive him."

To forgive does not mean we must remarry our ex-spouse; let prisoners out of jails; return to our old job, or anything else overt. The ego believes that if it forgives the one who has harmed it, it must translate this forgiveness into some behavior. But true forgiveness *requires* no bodily action, even though some gesture may perhaps accompany it. Forgiveness is an inner correction that lightens the heart. It is for our peace of mind first. Being at peace, we will now have peace to give to others, and this is the most permanent and valuable gift we can possibly give.

The root meaning of the verb *to forgive* is to let go. Forgiveness is a relinquishing of an unhelpful train of thought, a giving back to the ego that which is now recognized as undesirable. Forgiveness is a gentle refusal to defend ourselves against love any longer. It sees that all things are forgiving. It is a willingness to perceive everyone, including ourselves, as either expressing love or feeling a need for love. Any form of attack is a call for help, and the answer to every call for help is gentleness.

Forgiveness, like every other spiritual quality we have mentioned in this book—peace, love, equality, innocence, fearlessness, stillness, joy—does not imply a type of behavior. For example, to be *peaceful* does not imply that we must become "laid back"; to be *loving* does not require that we adopt certain mannerisms and a particular tone of voice; to recognize our spiritual *equality* with others does not mean it is desirable to lower ourselves to their ego level; to see our own *guiltlessness* is not to continue repeating our past mistakes; to be *fearless* we do not have to place ourselves or others in danger; to practice mental *quietness* we need not react to the world by fleeing from it; and to be *happy* does not mean we turn instead to an anxious form of ego excitement. Likewise, practicing forgiveness does not imply we must tell people we forgive them or act holier-than-thou around them. In attitudinal healing, the changing of our attitudes may result in certain changes in the way we act, but we usually recognize them in retrospect, and we do not make modifying our behavior our first priority.

This may appear to contradict an earlier statement I made that after pausing in peace we should act with assurance. But to say that it is better to do all we do in confidence is not to specify *what* action should be taken confidently. It is also better to act from love and peace, yet this must apply to *all* activities. Any decision made and carried out in the spirit of true forgiveness will bless everyone it touches and will not harm anyone.

Mother Teresa has been an inspiration to me for a number of years. Her words and example have supplied me with a gentle and needed correction on more than one occasion, and recently she, without knowing it, again taught me an important lesson. The stand she took at the Transpersonal Association Conference in India in February of 1982 was a clear and loving example of true forgiveness.

The conference was on the general theme of world peace, and Fritz Capra, one of the speakers, circulated a statement opposing the nuclear arms race and asked the other speakers if they would sign. I agreed to, as did a number of the others. But when Fritz asked Mother Teresa, she prayed and answered that she would not be able to. "If I signed," she said, "I would be loving some people and not others because I would be taking sides in a controversy." Baba Muktananda also declined to sign, and made the following statement: "There is no reason for a human to be afraid of the nuclear arms race. God has kept all three powers, birth, death and protection, in his Name. He hasn't handed them over to an individual. Even in the future He won't do it. I have complete confidence in that."

True forgiveness is based on reality. It overlooks the evidence gathered in from the point of view of a single body and turns instead to universal truth. The truth of our reality is that each of us is innocent and loved completely by God. It's not that we haven't made countless mistakes and will probably continue to do so for some time. But true forgiveness distinguishes between the deep urges of the heart and the more superficial desires of the ego. All mistakes come from the ego and are part of a learning process that everyone must go through. Forgiveness is a gentle vision that sees the maturity, the goodness of heart, and wholeness of character that will come in time to each person. And it recognizes the inappropriateness of condemnation to this growth process.

INTOLERANCE IS A FAILURE TO SEE

It is not just people we must forgive. Grievances can be held against cities, certain animals, a particular season of the year, foods, styles of dress, in fact anything the body's eyes see can become a source of unhappiness and even pain if we are intolerant of it. When Sharon Winter first came to the Center she was seventeen. Like many children, she had sensed the gravity of her condition before her doctor made his diagnosis. Her opinion had not been taken seriously, and Sharon had gone untreated for over a year before new tests were ordered and the cancerous condition known as lymphosarcoma was discovered. For this and several other reasons, by the time she reached our center she was very angry with the medical establishment and was suspicious of us.

At the time of her first visit, we had just one group of children, starting at age five. Sharon really didn't think she could learn anything from young kids, although at her first meeting she was surprised to see how happy everyone was. She suspected that even this was put on for her benefit. What amazed her most, however, was that an eight-year-old girl named Andrea, who had leukemia, was able to help her deal with her fear of an upcoming bone marrow procedure. Andrea suggested that she could take her mind completely off it by picturing herself on a beach in Hawaii, basking in the sun. She added, "You have to imagine it like you believe it one hundred percent." Sharon later did exactly as her young teacher instructed and to her amazement her fear and pain were minimal.

Before I continue with Sharon's story, I would like to expand a little on how mental imagery works, because there are many who might read the above paragraph and think that what Andrea said was so childish and overly simplistic as to be virtually useless to adults. Unfortunately, this is often true, not because mental imagery games are ineffective but because most adults will not try such a simple and direct approach.

Anything that can be stated as a concept can also be acted out in the imagination. Forgiveness, for example, is the exercise of our capacity to forget. We forget it because it is not worth thinking about. We forget it because to continue to remember it weakens us and makes us miserable. For many, a mental image such as the one I suggest in *Love Is Letting Go of Fear*, of filling a garbage can with our problems, attaching a helium balloon and watching it all float out of sight, can allow the mind to concentrate a little longer and thereby go a little deeper. A simple imagery such as seeing the light of God shine down upon the pain or the event, watching it surround it and dissolve it until there is nothing left but His light, can do much to release the mind of distress. The power is not in the particular imagery used but in our willingness to do something *now* to regain our peace.

As the months went by, Sharon went into remission, grew her hair back, recommenced her education, and eventually fell in love with a fine young man whom she later married. However, a little over a year ago, after we all thought everything was going so well for her, Sharon, now twenty-one, suffered a recurrence of cancer. Her faith in her doctor, the world and God were severely shaken. All her old anger toward the medical establishment returned as she faced multiple tests, new chemotherapy, losing her hair and, most of all, the uncertainty of the outcome.

She finally agreed to return to the hospital she so hated to resume treatment. On the day of her scheduled discharge, she was eager to go home. But that morning, a fifteen-year-old girl entered the hospital and was put in the bed next to Sharon. The girl's story was a most pathetic one. She had been abandoned by her parents and was going from one friend's home to another. Although suffering from Hodgkin's disease, she was terrified about the after-effects of chemotherapy and hadn't made up her mind whether to stay in the hospital or sign herself out. Sharon, despite her personal eagerness to leave now that her own treatment series was over, decided to stay in her bed an extra day as if nothing had happened, just so she could be there to help this new young friend. When her doctor discovered she had not checked out, he came into her room and asked her what was going on. When she told him the story, for the first time, she saw her doctor cry.

Intolerance, even intolerance of institutions such as hospitals, police departments, school administrations and government bureaus, is a failure to see beyond the appearance. It is a thought drawn from the past and imposed on what is presently being seen and usually has very little to do with what is taking place this instant. Sharon's love for this young girl allowed her to see the situation clearly and to act effectively.

FORGIVENESS IS A CALM SEEING

Intolerance, like all loveless feelings—fear, impatience, jealousy, anger, depression and so on—does not need to be fought or even resisted. The purpose of attitudinal healing is not to make of the mind a battlefield. Negative feelings evaporate whenever they are looked at calmly and honestly. This process is often gradual. All that is needed is that a gentle *trying* to forgive be made whenever we feel a sense of willingness and pleasure in making the effort. To add one more grudging obligation to our life, the obligation to forgive, is to fail completely to understand that forgiveness is our door to happiness.

Any emotion or thought that distresses you will begin to lose its hold on your mind when it is examined peacefully. Behind every negative feeling is an ego request, and do not be afraid to listen to what it asks you to do, for when you see clearly what is being demanded of you, you will also see that *you* do not want to do it. In discovering your true will, you will discover also that you are love.

A good habit to cultivate is to pause whenever you are having difficulty releasing your mind from an upset and look directly and in detail at the contents of your mind. Only a fearful avoidance of your attack thoughts will appear to give them power over you. Nothing negative can stand before the light of peace. But do not make the mistake of getting caught up in *analyzing* the contents of your mind. For example, it will waste your time and will probably depress you to ask yourself when you started feeling this way, how long it has gone on, why do you keep making this same mistake, and what rule can you make to avoid feeling this way in the future. Instead, just look calmly at your unforgiving thoughts, whatever form they are presently taking, and hear them out. Let your fears tell you their insane tale about the future. Allow your anger to suggest its ridiculous course of action. And if you do this quietly and honestly, you will eventually laugh happily at the absurdity of it all, and proceed again in love. There is no destructive thought or feeling that can withstand a persistent gentleness.

About a year ago, we began working with a family who had a son, twelve years of age, who had brain cancer. From all appearances, he did not have much longer to live. One day, the boy's father called me and said he had been dismissed from his job, not for negligence, but because of a company-wide reorganization. He was furious at the company's insensitivity, for they were all aware of his son's illness. Now he was being forced to go out on interviews, and this was upsetting him not only because it was taking him away from his son, but because the people who were interviewing him were much younger and less experienced than he was. He asked me for any thought that might help.

I told him that if he wanted peace of mind, it was important to forgive the people where he had worked and also important to see that those who were interviewing him were not his enemies.

He had told me that he had another appointment for the next day, and so I suggested that this time he look calmly at the young interviewer who would be questioning him and see that he too was nervous. The interviewer would naturally be afraid of overlooking something and getting the wrong person for the job. If the one he hired did not work out, this could possibly jeopardize his own position. I told him that once he saw for himself that the interviewer was also scared he would understand that they had come together to bring each other peace, even if the interviewer himself did not recognize this. I suggested that he set a single goal, not to get the job, but to have peace of mind during the interview by extending his love and consideration to the interviewer.

He called me back the next night and said, "You know, Jerry, I don't have any idea whether they will take me, but I do know I felt better when I left that interview than I have felt in a long, long time." As it turned out, he did get the job and at a higher salary than his previous position. This, of course, is not what is important, because learning of the healing power of forgiveness cannot be compared to any other benefit in this life.

Forgiveness is possibly the concept most central to attitudinal healing and yet it is also the one most likely to be misunderstood. I have already said that true forgiveness is not the adopting of a morally superior position. Nor does it acknowledge someone else's cruelty and pronounce it acceptable, for to do this would be dishonest. Forgiveness *sees* that no real grounds for condemnation exist, and for that to happen, new grounds for innocence must be recognized. Certainly the person's behavior cannot be rationalized away. He did behave the way he behaved. Possibly another motivation can be attributed to his behavior, such as fear instead of selfishness, and although this can be a good first step, it is not sufficient in itself to allow us to see the splendor of God's light within him. Forgiveness is a gentle turning away from what we see with our body's eyes and a searching for the truth that lies beyond the individual's ego.

Most people understand that deep urges for goodness exist in everyone's heart no matter how overlayered they may be with guilt, defensiveness, dishonesty and inhumanity. Forgiveness looks past the more superficial motivations of the individual, no matter how extreme these may be, to the place in his heart where he yearns for exactly what we yearn for. Everyone wants peace and safety. Everyone wants to make a difference. And everyone wants to release his potential for love. It is deep into this desire that forgiveness gazes, and seeing there a reflection of itself, it releases the other from judgment.

CHAPTER TWELVE
THE EXAMPLE OF LOVE

The Aberi family differed from the other families at the Center in two ways: a boy was born to the mother, Mary, after it was discovered she had cancer, and the grandparents were actively involved with the Center as well, so that we were relating to three generations. Of all the families I have worked with, perhaps none has given me such an in-depth experience with the various stages of life. They taught me a new perspective on birth and death as well as on parenting and grandparenting. The opportunity to become part of this extended family was one of the most meaningful experiences of my life.

Mary Aberi was a person whose life exemplified everything I have said to you in this book. Her love extended, and is still extending, to many people.

Mary was referred to me by her physician when she was thirty years old. At the time of our meeting, her son, Matty, was one and a half and was sunlight personified. Her husband, George, a manager at IBM, was handsome, sensitive and full of love.

She and George had waited eight years before she conceived,

and her pregnancy was a cause of much celebration. During the early months, her natural beauty and vitality became even more accentuated. Then, in the sixth month, cancer of the breast was diagnosed and, in the seventh, a mastectomy was performed. A bone scan was negative and the prognosis was optimistic.

Matty, a very healthy baby, was delivered by Caesarian surgery. He was so beautiful and radiant that some of their friends called him "the Christ child." Part of Mary's heart was exuberant with joy, but another part was frightened that she might not live long enough to see her son grow up and see the fruition of all the things she dreamed for him.

Until Matty was about six months of age, Mary seemed to be doing quite well, but then the cancer spread to her bones. Chemotherapy was started and she lost her hair. She began to experience pain, which medication did not seem to help. There was now great apprehension among the family members and it was at this time that she was referred to me.

On our first meeting, I felt drawn into Mary's light. She was spiritually luminescent, and I knew immediately she was going to be a significant teacher to me. Feelings of inner beauty, peace and unconditional love just seemed to radiate from her. I can't adequately describe the experience.

Initially, we met in my office twice a week, and she attended the Center's Tuesday night adult healing group. As time went on and her physical condition worsened, I saw her almost daily at home, and when I didn't see her we talked on the phone. I learned that as a young adult she had strayed from her religion and, because of the seeming unfairness of her current problems, was now having some mental battles with God. We became close spiritual partners and psychotherapists to each other. Mary would tell me her problems and I would tell her mine. Later, a great deal of our time together was spent praying. We became witnesses to the light of God in each other even when we were having trouble seeing it in ourselves. And the rest of the Aberi family took me in as well. I often joined them for meals, played with Matty, loved and received love from George and from Matty's grandparents.

Patsy Robinson, Carleita Schwartz, Jonelle Simpson and many others from our Person-to-Person Program visited Mary regularly. Each, in her own way, commented that she came away having received more than she had given. No one could really articulate what happened in her presence, but I do know that we all experienced the peace of God.

Mary became active in our telephone network. She gave courage, hope and love in abundance and helped others deal with their pain, while also learning to use attitudinal healing to lessen her own discomfort. There was a quality in her voice that filled the listener with peace, even over the phone.

During this period, a young woman, Shari Podersky, came from Vancouver to see me because of a brain tumor she had developed, and I suggested she visit Mary. When she came back, she said she didn't need a plane to fly home, she was so high. Later, Shari also began to give help over the phone. The linkage she experienced with Mary unfolded like a circle of love, always extending and expanding.

I remember one evening in the hospital when Mary was receiving large doses of morphine every four hours for the severe pain. I found her sleeping when I arrived, so I just held her hand in silence and prayed. Suddenly, the phone rang. The operator said it was an emergency call for me. It was a man in Wyoming with cancer of the lung who was in pain and asking for help. The phone had awakened Mary and she heard my conversation. She asked to talk to him. As she shared her love and gave him some simple imageries to use, I saw the blood rushing back into her cheeks and, for that moment, she was the picture of health.

Six months later when she was hospitalized again, she had a roommate, a woman who was dying of cancer and probably had no more than a few days to live. When I arrived, Mary asked me to talk with the woman and her family. I forget what I said, but I do remember what they said. They told me they felt Mary was truly an angel and that just being and talking with her had helped them let go of their fear and despair.

Possibly more than anyone I have known, Mary chose not to

identify with her body. Instead, she believed in spiritual reality as her true being and she understood the importance of living in the present. Thus, she had a sense of peace that was conveyed to everyone around her. In giving peace, she was able to experience it herself. She was a living demonstration of the principle that to give is to receive.

Of the many things Mary and I taught each other, the most significant was that words are not necessary. The best moments we spent together were the silent ones, with joined hands and in prayer, giving gratitude for being in God's presence and feeling the infinity of His peace and love. As her trust in God increased, her peace radiated, and her family began to feel their fears dissipate.

One night, I left Mary's house about 10:30 P.M. Although she was weak, she could talk and was very peaceful. About 2:00 A.M., I received a call from George who said that she had gone into a coma. I went back to the house immediately. The whole family was there. I knew what God and Mary wanted me to do. I was to share my own peace with everyone, to see her light and to not identify with her body. I knew that she had waited so I could be there to help her family through this transition. Mary died at 4:00 A.M.

One week later, we had a celebration of life at our Center in honor of Mary. Jeanne Carter, a staff member, said, "I used to go up and see Mary at lunchtime when I was having a difficult day, and she had a remarkable ability to see right to the center of a situation, to get rid of all the garbage and junk, and in such a gentle and loving manner, to help me see that everything was really okay. I would always come back feeling very happy, very light and full of joy. She had a remarkable gift for clearing away all the nonessentials, and when you got down to the core of the problem, there was nothing there. She was a beautiful person.

"One day my daughter, Janet, was visiting and Mary wanted to meet her. She wasn't really receiving new people but she wanted to meet Janet, so I drove her over and we went in. Mary was losing her hair again, was swollen and, if you just looked at the body, I guess she wasn't very pretty, but her radiance was beautiful. When we left, I resisted the temptation to ask my daughter what she thought of Mary because everybody thought so much of her, but Janet said spontaneously, 'She is the most beautiful woman I have ever seen,' and that was all you saw in Mary—her beauty."

Another staff member, Patsy Robinson, in reference to Shari Podersky's visit which I mentioned earlier, had this to say:

"So Mary sat there and talked to this woman and I just listened. It was as if God was speaking through Mary. She was saying the most beautiful things to Shari and there was a—we use the word 'transformation,' and maybe we use it too lightly—but I saw with my eyes; I saw this woman transformed from such a fearful state into a peaceful state. And Mary's peace was extending to me also. And Shari's mother and father were sitting on a piano bench, listening, and suddenly her father leaned over and touched me. Mary was engrossed at this point, talking to Shari. He had tears in his eyes as he said, 'I don't believe what's happening.' "

Shari expressed her feelings this way:

"Well, my first introduction to Mary was quite by surprise. Patsy said there was this wonderful, marvelous person that I'd have to meet and she phoned Mary who said we could come up. My mom and dad and I went to see her.

"We walked in and she greeted us. Her little boy was asleep in the playpen. I walked into her room and it was completely peaceful. And for me—I get very emotional talking about it—it was the first time that I was ever in a really peaceful place. I wasn't very peaceful myself at that time. Then she sat down and just started talking and teaching. She glowed all the time. I think it was the most moving experience I ever had. I don't know what else to tell you. I think that she is beautiful."

That day, we phoned John in Wyoming. John was the emergency caller Mary talked with the night I was in her room at the hospital. About Mary, he's said:

"From Mary I learned that everything has its purpose, although we may not understand it. That everything is okay. I often called her when I was really down and she just had a way of responding that would help me see that the universe is in order and that the things that were happening to both of us were not tragic.

Sometimes we even talked about funerals and, not trying to be silly or anything, we'd end up laughing about the whole concept of dying and how important it was for us to have a nice funeral—without being morbid, you know.

"The first conversation I had with her in the room there, we seemed to click—I don't know whether psychically or spiritually—and it was as if two old friends who hadn't seen one another in a long time had just been reunited. As our relationship developed, we seemed to call one another at times when both of us needed to talk and had been thinking of each other. Mary had a way of saying, 'John, you're my teacher. I learn so much from you.' And she enabled me to have some hope."

It has been over a year now since Mary died. I see Matty, George and Matty's grandparents frequently. Sometimes it is not easy. There are riptides of grief for all of us. Mary's presence, however, continues to be felt.

A FINAL NOTE

As I was writing about Mary, my son, Lee, phoned. Mary was Lee's teacher also. I told him how difficult it was to put the essence of Mary into words and he made the following suggestion: "Why don't you say just that? And when you come to the end of Mary's story, ask the reader to put the book down for a few minutes, close his eyes, and let his own mind be still and experience the essence of Mary."

So that is what I am doing. Mary is love and love will come to you. As you experience her light and her warmth, know they are the coming of your real self in God.

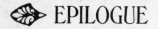 # EPILOGUE

To me, Mary Aberi epitomizes attitudinal healing. She did her utmost to not just think *about* God but to allow God's light to pour through her for all to behold and partake. She chose not to identify with her body, not to identify with her ego personality. She demonstrated that as long as we are breathing we are here on earth to be a channel for God's blessing, to be centered only on love, and in that way to be of service to others. She somehow knew that death is illusory and that life is eternal. She knew that the mind is not confined to the body and that life and the body are not the same. This was more than a belief with Mary. It was a conviction deep in her heart that inspired conviction in others.

Mary made alive two simple statements from *A Course in Miracles* that have become of central importance to me.

1. Awaken and forget all thoughts about death, and you will find that you have the peace of God.
2. Today I will let Christ's vision look upon all things for me and judge them not, but I will give each one the miracle of love instead.

Mary and the others I have spoken of in this book have demonstrated that there is nothing in the material world as important as the love of God in our hearts. To allow a gradual and ever increasing release of that love is our only function.

Let us gently and quietly and frequently remind ourselves that our true mind contains only God's thoughts—thoughts of love and peace. When there are other thoughts, we have manufactured them ourselves, and therefore we can decide to release them ourselves. This requires no struggle, only the recognition that we would rather be happy than right. It is these other thoughts, these judgments and justifications, that lead us to believe that what our physical senses tell us is what has meaning. These thoughts construct around us a world where we are destined to die, a world that is filled with despair, a world in which we are in constant danger of being attacked or abandoned, a world where we are separate from each other and from God. But such a world is not reality.

Let us now choose to forgive the world, to forgive our bodies, and all those we see. Let us decide to live in the real world of God's love and to have our own internal light shine on everything with a blaze of glory. Let us experience the joy that comes from letting go of our fears, our guilts and embarrassments, our grievances and bitter hopes. Let us be quiet just an instant and experience the nearness of God. Know that He loves us all with boundless and endless love. Let us be still just one instant and allow God to come to us and bring us back into the center of His heart. Let us now have love, happiness and certainty of purpose. May the unimportant *be* unimportant forevermore. And may that ancient memory of who and what and where we are rise in our hearts until all this world's pain be gone.

Peace be to us all.